Sept 2002

WISDOM
FROM THE
ROBBER BARONS

WISDOM
FROM THE
ROBBER BARONS

ENDURING BUSINESS LESSONS FROM
ROCKEFELLER, MORGAN,
AND THE FIRST INDUSTRIALISTS

GEORGE DAVID SMITH
AND
FREDERICK DALZELL

PERSEUS PUBLISHING

Cambridge, Massachusetts

Copyright © 2000 by The Winthrop Group

A CIP catalog record for this book is available from the Library of Congress.
ISBN 0-7382-0372-6

Perseus Publishing is a member of the Perseus Books Group.

Find us on the World Wide Web at http://www.perseuspublishing.com

Perseus Publishing books are available at special discounts for bulk purchases in the U.S. by corporations, institutions, and other organizations. For more information, please contact the Special Markets Department at HarperCollins Publishers, 10 East 53rd Street, New York, NY 10022, or call 1-212-207-7528.

Text design by Jeff Williams
Set in 11-point Minion by Perseus Publishing Services

First printing, September 2000
1 2 3 4 5 6 7 8 9 10—03 02 01 00

CONTENTS

Preface   vii
Introduction:
Why the Robber Barons Matter   *ix*

1 Venturing   *1*

2 Competing   *35*

3 Managing   *67*

4 Leading   *89*

Chronology:
Business and World Events, 1870–1929   *113*

Further Reading   *127*

Index   *131*

PREFACE

We knew that compiling a handy reference of quotable wisdom from the "Robber Barons" would be fun, but also tricky. The great entrepreneurs of the industrial age—John D. Rockefeller, J.P. Morgan, and Henry Ford, for example—were the Shakespeares, Rembrandts, and Mozarts of industry. They laid the groundwork for the modern world economy, after all, and many of their ideas about entrepreneurship, organizational design, and leadership were not only original and compelling when they were first articulated, they've stood the test of time.

We wanted to do something different with their words. What differentiates this volume from prior books on business quotations is that we have taken what we think are the principal players' most important insights and have threaded them through a running commentary, in order to make clearer the larger social and economic implications of their ideas.

We thank Nick Philipson, our editor, for helping us understand what we needed to do to make this book vivid as well as edifying. We thank our colleagues at The Winthrop Group, Inc., serious historians all, for supporting our effort with their suggestions about themes and insights. In the end, we hope that this volume entertains, and in the process whets an appetite for further reading into the lives and ideas of the great business leaders who created the world we live in today.

G.D. Smith
F. Dalzell

INTRODUCTION: WHY THE ROBBER BARONS MATTER

My ideas of business are no doubt old-fashioned, but the fundamental principles do not change from generation to generation, and sometimes I think that our quick-witted American business-men, whose spirit and energy are so splendid, do not always sufficiently study the real underlying foundations of business management.

—JOHN D. ROCKEFELLER

New networks spread across the landscape in an intricate web, carrying information and freight across continents and over oceans with astonishing speed. The pace of business accelerates sharply, and markets that had been dispersed, isolated islands rapidly coalesce into new interdependent economic systems, new global configurations. Dazzling new technologies transform material lives. New media flourish, new industries emerge seemingly overnight. The breadth, the depth, the rate of change is exhilarating, and profoundly unsettling too. The gap separating the rich and the poor grows wider. Investor speculation runs rampant. Businesses rise and fall. Broad swathes of the workforce are mowed down; entire occupations are downsized out of existence. At the same time, brash new entrepreneurs collect vast new fortunes. The scramble for wealth transfixes the popular imagination. Everyone knows the world will never be the same again.

Sound familiar? It should. That scenario suits our own times, of course. But it also describes the era of business indelibly stamped by legendary entrepreneurs like John D. Rockefeller, Andrew Carnegie, and J. P. Morgan. Roughly one hundred years before the emergence of the "New Economy," an earlier generation of industrialists built a new economy of their own. Over a period running from the 1870s through the 1920s, the United States—and the world—underwent fundamental and far-reaching transformations. At the heart of the economy, industrial production and distribution on a massive scale supplanted agriculture, craft industries, and traditional commerce. It became the age of the so-called Robber Barons.

Everyone knows the names. Rockefeller, Carnegie, Vanderbilt, Duke, Morgan, Ford, Du Pont, and Sloan have become a part of the business and cultural landscapes—by virtue of the charities and universities they endowed, if nothing else, or the mansions they cobbled together.

We tend to dismiss their businesses, however, as "Old Economy," moldy "bricks and mortar," lumbering "dinosaurs," dusty relics. As one curmudgeon once said:

" History is more or less bunk. It's tradition. We don't want tradition. We want to live in the present and the only history that is worth a tinker's damn is the history we make today. "

HENRY FORD

So why listen to voices like Ford's now that they too have passed into history? Because whether they valued history or not, they created a world the rest of us need to know about. They ventured, and competed, and built their businesses in circumstances that are in many respects strikingly similar to those of the present day. Whether they know it or not, chip makers, telecom empire builders, and dot.com visionaries have inherited the legacy forged by people like Ford, Rockefeller, and Carnegie.

During the golden age of industry, running from the midnineteenth century through 1930 or so, the Robber Barons commercialized risky high technologies and figured out how to build radically new organizations from the bottom up. They identified the great entrepreneurial and management issues of the world's first big business corporations, and they devised surprisingly durable solutions to the basic business problems of modern civilization. Their ideas about taking and controlling risk, creating wealth, building organizations, managing growth, and causing and coping with social and economic change have, at times, a remarkably modern ring to them. Their experience, in short, remains profoundly relevant.

Of course, not all verities are eternal. As the food-processing magnate J. Ogden Armour once quipped: "Some axioms are true; others aren't." What could be truer than that? Yet the experience of the great industrialists, people who changed their world as much as Bill Gates, Jeff Bezos, and Michael Milken are changing ours, continues to ring true. The entrepreneurs and enterprises of the Industrial Age have compelling business lessons for our own postindustrial era.

I

VENTURING

*The Edison Company offered me the general su-
perintendency of the company but only on condition that I would give up my gas engine and
devote myself to something really useful. I had to
choose between my job and my automobile. . . . I
quit my job on August 15, 1899, and went into the
automobile business.*

—HENRY FORD, *MY LIFE AND WORK*, 1922

The great entrepreneurs of the Industrial Age were a diverse lot.
But they also had a lot in common, with each other and with
their counterparts in our own era. First and foremost, they ventured. As they looked at the world around them, they saw possibilities where others saw problems and pitfalls. They took the
risks necessary to develop new products, new services, and new
ways of doing business.

Like entrepreneurs today, they ventured in an environment of
revolutionary technological and economic change. By the 1880s a
new infrastructure of railroad lines and telegraph wires was "net-
working" the country and the world. The United States, once a
scattered collection of island communities, was knitting itself together into a single national market. People were moving from the

farms to the cities, and immigrants were flowing in to take advantage of the new job opportunities created by industrial activity.

A few entrepreneurs managed not just to ride out these changes but to drive them. Maybe they were especially resourceful, or particularly lucky. Probably they were both. The jarring social and economic dislocation made for a profoundly disorienting environment in which to try to do business. But it was also a profoundly exhilarating period—a time when business was expanding and reconfiguring into enterprises broader and grander than anything that had been assembled before.

Fundamentally, the great venturers of the industrial era were the ones who learned how to steer within the gale force winds of what Joseph Schumpeter called "creative destruction." They did not always know where they were headed. They had no precedents to work from, no models for their ventures. So they improvised. And when their improvised solutions created new problems, they improvised some more. Ultimately, they learned to cope with change and to become comfortable with it—or at least to accept that it was riskier in the end to resist change than it was to embrace it.

Expecting Change: A Parable

> The man who is too set to change is dead already. The funeral is a mere detail.
>
> HENRY FORD

Ford said it again and again, with contempt for those who remained complacent:

> Stability is a dead fish floating downstream. The only kind of stability we know in this country is change.
>
> HENRY FORD

And with urgency for the coming generation of businesspeople:

> My advice to young men is to be ready to revise any system, scrap any methods, abandon any theory if the success of the job requires it.
>
> HENRY FORD, *MY PHILOSOPHY OF INDUSTRY*, 1929

It is not in my disposition to stop and pin medals on myself. But any one who does business with Mr. Ford never gets a chance to rest and enjoy honours. The pressure for better methods is continuous.

Harvey Firestone (one of Ford's suppliers),
***Men and Rubber*, 1926**

Ford knew what he was talking about. After all, he built his business on the principle, taking a product no one considered to be suitable to mass production and rigorously applying new methods of manufacturing until he learned how to make it efficiently enough to price it for mainstream American consumption.

Behind that accomplishment lay a willingness to reimagine the world around him. When, as a young man, Ford wheeled his first car—he called it a "quadricycle"—before his family, they were dubious. His father would not ride in the contraption at first. His sister later recalled:

> It was characteristic of Father that he would not ride in the car on that first day. He was as interested as all

of us in the fact that here was the horseless carriage about which we had been hearing. He looked it all over and listened with interest to Henry's explanation of it, but he refused to ride in it. At that time I think all of us shared Father's feeling that here was but another interesting toy which Henry had built. I know we all wondered about its practical significance. After all, we had some fine horses of which all of us were very proud. . . . That first little car, while it ran, seemed to us to be a pitifully small thing indeed. We wondered how it could have caused Henry to leave his good farm and financial security just to be able to build this thing. Father was a conservative farmer of those times. He saw no reason why he should risk his life at that time for a brief thrill from being propelled over the road in a carriage without horses. He liked his horses and was proud of them. They did a better job at that time than did Henry's little car.

MARGARET FORD RUDDIMAN

It will take a hundred years to tell whether [Ford] helped us or hurt us, but he certainly didn't leave us where he found us.

Will Rogers

No wonder Ford needled those around him about staying open to change. He had to keep after them, to bring them around to the business possibilities he saw.

There was no "demand" for automobiles—there never is for a new article.

HENRY FORD, *MY LIFE AND WORK*, 1922

But then Ford himself proved just as vulnerable to the next round of change. He stubbornly resisted technological and marketing innovations pioneered by his competitors at General Motors, lost market leadership, and very nearly ruined his business. Just as the horse-and-buggy was driven off the road by the automobile, Ford's sturdy Model T was swept aside by GM's more fashionable model changes. Now it was his competitor's turn to remind a rising new generation of entrepreneurs:

> " There have been and always will be many opportunities to fail in the automobile industry. The circumstances of the ever-changing market and ever-changing product are capable of breaking any business organization if that organization is unprepared for change—indeed, in my opinion, if it has not provided procedures for anticipating change. "

ALFRED SLOAN, *MY YEARS WITH GENERAL MOTORS*, 1964

To which the head of R&D at GM in the 1920s added:

> " The world hates change, yet it is the only thing that has brought progress. "

CHARLES F. "BOSS" KETTERING

Carnegie and Chemistry:
Change as a Constant Pressure

So it went. Rapid change had become the one constant in the postagrarian world. The quotidian rhythms of the seasons had been displaced by the hurly-burly of competitive progress. Every new product was a threat to an old one. Every new way of doing business was a threat to some vested interest. No one could afford to relax. Those who mastered new techniques for transforming old businesses pushed hundreds of older competitors out of the market. The horse gave way to the horseless carriage, and then Ford's Model T gave way to a phalanx of GM cars in market segment formation. Electricity washed away all the hard work of those who had built gas lighting systems. Investments in the telegraph were eroded by the telephone.

Mastering technological change, in particular, had become a vital condition of doing business.

> Little, I think, does one know, who is not in the whirlwind of business affairs, of the rarity of the combined qualities requisite for conducting the business enterprise of today. The time has passed when business once established can be considered almost permanently secure. Business methods have changed; good will counts for less and less. Success in business is held . . . nowadays . . . at the cost of perpetual challenge to all comers.
>
> ANDREW CARNEGIE

Carnegie talked from experience. The steel magnate closely followed developments in metallurgy and decisively adopted new methods. He did not invent the Bessemer steel process, for example; he was not even the first American steelmaker to try it out. But once he was convinced it made steel more efficiently, Carnegie made a total commitment to the new technology, building massive new steel mills to take advantage of it.

> What others could not or would not do we would attempt, and this was a rule of business which was strictly adhered to.
>
> ANDREW CARNEGIE, *AUTOBIOGRAPHY*, 1920

Of course, he courted risks. But like other great venturers, Carnegie was not so much risk-prone as prone to minimize the risks that others saw. In 1872 he put *all* the money he had earned in railroads and other businesses into steel, confident in the competitive leverage the new technologies offered. There were already lots of experienced companies in the iron and steel business, but Carnegie knew he had found an edge.

> I am sure that any competent judge would be surprised how little I ever risked. . . . My supply of Scotch caution [was] the responsible party. My supply of Scotch caution was never small.
>
> ANDREW CARNEGIE, *AUTOBIOGRAPHY*, 1920

> I never gamble.
>
> **J. P. Morgan**

And critically, as his business expanded, Carnegie learned how to incorporate continuous technological innovation into his enterprise. He hired chemists and set up experimental laboratories at his mills, pioneering the principle of corporate research and development.

> It was years after we had taken chemistry to guide us that it was said by the proprietors of some other furnaces that they could not afford to employ a chemist. Had they known the truth then, they would have known that they could not afford to be without one.
>
> ANDREW CARNEGIE, *AUTOBIOGRAPHY*, 1920

Or, as he put the lesson most memorably:

" Nine-tenths of all the uncertainties of pig-iron making were dispelled under the burning sun of chemical knowledge. "

ANDREW CARNEGIE, *AUTOBIOGRAPHY*, 1920

There never was a great character who did not sometimes smash the routine regulations and make new ones for himself.

Andrew Carnegie

The Capacity for Vision

" There could be no progress until enough people could be made dissatisfied—and this could be done only when they were brought to think beyond the limits to which they were accustomed. "

THOMAS EDISON

I never attempted to systematize Edison's business life. Edison's whole method of work would upset the system of any business office. He cared not for the hours of the day or the days of the week. I . . . would get at him whenever it suited his convenience. Sometimes he would not go over his mail for days at a time. I used more often to get at him at night than in the day time, as it left my days free to transact his affairs.

Samuel Insull, Edison's partner

Edison is enshrined in the popular historical imagination as America's most prolific inventor. He was also one of the Industrial Age's most important entrepreneurs, founding a string of companies, including several firms that consolidated as General Electric. In Menlo Park, Edison fashioned the Silicon Valley of his day, a high-tech hotbed and, for Edison himself, a place to cultivate his unique capacity for seeing what others missed.

Edison's Laboratory

The average person's brain does not observe a thousandth part of what the eye observes. . . . It is almost incredible how poor our powers of observation—genuine observation—are. Let me give an illustration: When we first started the incandescent lighting system we had a lamp factory at the bottom of a hill, at Menlo Park. It was a very busy time for us all. Seventy-five of us worked twenty hours every day and slept only four hours—and thrived on it. I fed them all, and I had a man play an organ all the time we were at work. One midnight, while at lunch, a matter came up which caused me to refer to a cherry tree beside the hill leading from the main works to the lamp factory. Nobody seemed to know anything about the location of the cherry tree. This made me conduct a little investigation, and I found that although twenty-seven of these men had used this path every day for six months not one of them had ever noticed the tree.

THOMAS EDISON

Name the greatest of all inventors: Accident.

Mark Twain

I never did anything worth doing by accident.

THOMAS EDISON

The Rigors of Invention

When an interviewer asked Edison in 1890 which of his hundreds of inventions had taken the most experimentation, Edison promptly answered: "The electric light."

Just consider this: we have an almost infinitesimal filament heated to a degree which it is difficult for us to comprehend, and it is in a vacuum, under conditions of which we are wholly ignorant. You cannot use your eyes to help you in the investigation, and you really know nothing of what is going on in that tiny bulb. I speak without exaggeration when I say that I have constructed three thousand different theories in connection with the electric light, each one of them reasonable and apparently likely to be true. Yet only in two cases did my experiments prove the truth of my theory.

Ultimately Edison proved to be an indifferent businessman. But as a venturer, he was supreme. For though he lacked any inclination for bookkeeping or methodical management, Edison had vision—and without vision no business could (or can) survive change.

Telecom: Nurturing a Vision

Alexander Graham Bell had it too. As early as 1878, Bell foresaw the day when the telephone—then capable of transmitting speech only over very short distances—would become technologically capable of competing with the telegraph. Addressing a group of financial backers in London Bell proclaimed:

> I believe that in the future wires will unite the head offices of Telephone Companies in different cities, and a man in one part of the country may communicate by word of mouth with another in a different place.
>
> ALEXANDER GRAHAM BELL

> The telephone reminds me of a child only it grows much more rapidly. What is before it in the future, no man can tell—but I see new possibilities before it—and new uses.
>
> **Alexander Graham Bell, 1876**

In hindsight, Bell's vision of what form the new technology would take was prophetic: he saw "telephony" becoming "telecom." But the vision was so radical when he first uttered it that even Bell's financial backers were skeptical. For that matter, so was Bell's most serious rival, the Western Union Telegraph monopoly, which passed on an opportunity to buy his telephone patents for $100,000. To Western Union's president, William Orton, the new technology looked like nothing more than a "toy."

Bell and his backers were forced to go into business for themselves. Through intense effort they eventually laid the foundation for what would become the world's greatest telecommunications system—and incidentally purchased Western Union along the way.

American Union Telephone Company Stock

So the head of AT&T was imparting hard-won wisdom in 1910 when he explained in the company's annual report:

> " The original idea upon which may be founded great development may be revolutionary but it never springs full-fledged or perfect into the world. . . . To develop the business it was first necessary to develop the "art." It was unique, nothing like it existed; the whole art of the practical application of electricity was new and undeveloped. "
>
> THEODORE VAIL

By the time Vail reached this understanding he had worked for years within AT&T, quit in frustration, then returned when the company was reorganized with new financial backing. He came back because he was determined to build the telephone and the company into the platform for a vision he never lost sight of:

> One system with a common policy, common purpose and common action; comprehensive, universal, interdependent, intercommunicating like the highway system of the country, extending from every door to every other door, affording electrical communication of every kind, from every one at every place to every one at every other place.
>
> THEODORE VAIL

To draw an analogy, what AT&T eventually managed to accomplish represented something roughly equivalent to what it took the federal government, Intel, Xerox PARC, Cisco, Netscape, and scores of other companies to create a century later: an Internet.

Making It Work

> The man with a new idea is a Crank until the idea succeeds.
>
> MARK TWAIN

Vision is one thing then, implementation another. Mark Twain, who invested in a series of failed ventures, learned that lesson firsthand.

Charles Schwab knew it too. Now, Schwab was no inventor. He was a hard-edged steel executive, first with Carnegie, then with J. P. Morgan's U.S. Steel, then as the head of Bethlehem Steel. He probably would have missed the cherry tree out in front of the factory; he might not have backed Bell or Vail. But he did share with those other venturers a capacity for seeing, thinking, and planning beyond the limits of the landscape in front of him.

> " A man to carry on a successful business must have imagination. He must see things as in a vision, a dream of the whole thing. "
>
> CHARLES SCHWAB

What Schwab was talking about was the ability not just to recognize opportunities but to envision how to execute, to map out the realization of the venture.

Consider, as an illustration, how potent a force Edison became in combination with J. P. Morgan, the preeminent American financier. As an investment banker, J. P. Morgan was generally conservative and cautious. His forte was the restructuring of mature businesses, and rather than plunge into a new venture, he preferred to hang back, waiting until a project had proven itself.

But he was powerfully drawn to Edison's vision of incandescent lighting. The inventor incorporated the Edison Electric Light Company in 1878, announcing grandly that he had devised technology capable of illuminating houses and cities via a system of electric lights running off a single power generator. Morgan wanted in. His bank, Drexel Morgan, took charge of the new venture's financing.

That steady backing proved critical as Edison and his engineers ran into a series of technical glitches that considerably stretched out both the timetable and the expense of the project. Some of Morgan's junior partners and a number of Edison's investors grew nervous. But Morgan remained committed, and when New York City's Pearl Street generator was finally switched on, it lit 106 electric lamps in the downtown offices of Drexel Morgan.

The banker even put his own house in the inventor's hands. Morgan's Manhattan mansion became the first residence in New York

City to be wired up for electric lighting. It proved to be a trying experience, though. Shortly after the system was up and running, faulty wiring set off a fire in Morgan's library, torching the banker's desk. Edison's chief lieutenant, Edward Johnson, hurried over to inspect the soggy, charred debris. As he poked through the pile, he later recalled, "Morgan appeared in the doorway with a newspaper in his hand, and looked at me over the tops of his glasses."

"Well?" the imposing man demanded. Johnson began to collect his thoughts, fashion something by way of excuse or explanation. Then he caught sight of Mrs. Morgan standing behind her husband. "She put her finger to her lips, then vanished down the hall," he remembered. Johnson said nothing. After a pause, Morgan asked what the engineer was going to do. Make the wiring safe, replied Johnson; the lights were fine, but the wiring had been faulty. Morgan took the reply in, studying Johnson. Then he asked how long it would take and told Johnson to begin right away.

Planting New Products

Sometimes creating a new product proved as easy as obliging a customer. When bicycle manufacturer Alexander Winton approached Benjamin Franklin Goodrich about supplying pneumatic tires for a "horseless carriage" he was building, the rubber manufacturer agreed to work something up.

> " I guess we can make them, although we never have. "
> BENJAMIN FRANKLIN GOODRICH

That simple, workmanlike response launched the tire industry. But more often, new products emerged haltingly, through trial and error, with far more hits than misses. Applications rarely announced themselves so clearly. Consider the story of broadcast radio.

During World War I, Westinghouse built up a substantial business supplying radios for the military. Facing the prospect of peace, company strategists began casting about for new markets. In this frame of mind, Harry P. Davis noticed an advertisement in a Pittsburgh department store selling wireless radio sets. The ad informed buyers that they would be able to hear music over their sets, transmitted by a Westinghouse engineer, Frank Conrad. Conrad was transmitting the music from his house by simply pulling his Victrola up to his transmitter.

A revelation struck Davis.

> The efforts that were then being made to develop radio telephony as a confidential means of communication were wrong. Instead its field was really one of wide publicity.
>
> HARRY P. DAVIS

In November 1920 Westinghouse launched KDKA, the nation's first commercial radio station, and within the year the firm was selling receivers to a hungry market.

It had taken a sudden twist of perspective, a willingness to upend perceptions of the technology and the business opportunities it created. And the suggestion did not come through the usual channels. It was extracurricular and literally in the air, waiting for imagination and a new notion of application.

What Westinghouse identified, then nurtured, was a latent market need, one that customers might never have articulated for themselves.

A similar flash of insight hit King Gillette one morning in 1895. The traveling salesman was shaving with a dull straight razor when inspiration struck.

> As I stood there with my razor in my hand, my eyes resting on it as lightly as a bird settling down on its nest—the Gillette razor was born. I saw it all in a mo-

" ment, and in that moment many unvoiced questions were asked and answered more with the rapidity of a dream than by the slow process of reasoning. It seemed as though I could see the way the blade could be held in a holder; then came the idea of sharpening opposite edges on the thin piece of steel that was uniform in thickness throughout, thus doubling its services; and following in sequence came the clamping plates for the blades and a handle easily disposed between the two edges of the blade. All this came more in pictures than in thought as though the razor were a finished thing and held before my eyes. "

Fool that I was, I knew little about razors and practically nothing about steel, and I could not foresee the trials and tribulations that I was to pass through before the razor was a success.

KING GILLETTE

Years of development lay ahead for Gillette, who formed his company in 1901. He did not put his first razor on the market until 1903, selling a grand total of 51 razors and 168 blades in the first year of production. He would have to labor intensively and systematically over several years to engineer a product that would make his flash of inspiration manifest.

Historical Echo: Amazon.com and Montgomery Ward

The emergence of online commerce has begun to restructure retailing in fascinating and far-reaching ways. New "stores" are going up in cyberspace—such as eBay, Priceline, eToys, and Amazon.com—representing not just new businesses but new *kinds* of business. Entrepreneurs like Jeff

(continues)

(continued)

Bezos are trying to rechannel paths of distribution, refashion habits of consumption, and reinvent the structure of the retailing firm.

Bezos has a distant forefather in the man who assembled the first mass mail-order business, A. Montgomery Ward. He got off to a rough start. Ward launched his first catalog business in 1871 but was wiped out in the Great Chicago Fire. In 1872 he started again, issuing a one-page catalog listing 150 items for sale. Within a few years the catalog had grown to 72 pages, illustrated with wood-cut illustrations. By 1880 it was running over 500 pages, and Ward was employing 300 clerks to handle the hundreds of thousands of orders flooding in every year.

Selling through mail-order catalogs tapped powerful new market possibilities. Montgomery Ward offered unparalleled assortments of goods to rural customers whose purchasing patterns had been tethered to local general stores, which had high markups and limited stock selections. In a word, the mail-order catalog represented the portal of its era, opening unprecedented access to wide new ranges of consumption and experience.

Other parallels link Montgomery Ward and Amazon.com. Both had to pioneer the construction of new systems and new logistics. And most critically, both businesses had to build a new kind of relationship with customers. To build a new kind of *commerce,* Ward, like Bezos, sought to create a new kind of *community*. He had to figure out how to reestablish, on new footings, much of what he was taking apart. To counter the depersonalizing effect of lifting sales out of stores and eliminating direct, face-to-face contact between merchant and customer, Ward affiliated his business with the Grange movement—a network of rural farmers' cooperatives. And internally, he took pains to impress everyone within the firm with "the fact that we are doing business with people personally and not impersonally." He directed that all letters to customers "be personally written," in a style that embodied what he characterized as "the personality of the firm" as well as "the personality of the writer." He strove continuously to give each of his millions of customers, in sum, "the feeling that he or she is not buying from a big impersonal mail order establishment, but that we are still a personality or group of them, no matter how many millions the business may totalize."

> " We study methods of improving our business as we would a science. We imitate no one. "
>
> A. MONTGOMERY WARD

Creating New Markets

Customers for new kinds of products did not spring out of nowhere. Markets often had to be fabricated. As Henry Ford put it:

> " Purchasers are made, not born. "
>
> HENRY FORD

Contrary to one economic saw, supply did not necessarily create its own demand. This was especially true in a frontier society where taste and consumer habits required considerable cultivation. The retailer Potter Palmer, who was moving literally to the frontier when he went to Chicago in 1852, built an early version of the department store, expecting to capitalize on a rapidly growing urban population. It was certainly not a matter of waiting for something to happen.

> I always hunted for customers. If I learned a man was two hundred miles away in a clearing in the forest . . . I got the name of my establishment to him and invited him in. After he once got acquainted with the store, we rarely lost him.
>
> POTTER PALMER

Henry Ford, of course, built his business by proactively redefining the automotive market, well in advance of any defined demand for an inexpensive car. In 1908, when he made his first Model T, automobiles were expensive luxury items. That first-year model cost $850. But it was durable and designed to be as simple to manufacture as Ford could make it. Once he had his product he went to work on his production process, reengineering it repeatedly, with a single-minded intensity that steadily reduced his production costs and prices. By 1924 the Model T cost $290, even as inflation had risen dramatically, and Ford had put more than 10 million of them on the roads. The automobile had become something much more basic and far more common than a luxury. Ford had indeed managed to "make" his purchasers.

> We took what was a luxury and turned it into a necessity. Our only advantage was lack of precedent.
>
> HENRY FORD

Economic efficiency consists of making things worth more than they cost.

Economist John Maurice Clark

Making necessities of luxuries is precisely what most great entrepreneurs of the Industrial Age were up to. Cultivating markets took as much work, as much imagination, as much vision, as inventing new technologies. Ford did it by lowering costs. Other venturers did it by stimulating markets. Consider the case of aluminum.

Aluminum, an aesthetically pleasing, silvery metal, is light, durable, rust-free, corrosion-resistant, a fine reflector, and a good conductor of heat and electricity. Yet, despite its abundance as an element in the earth, it was extremely difficult and costly to liberate from its oxide-bound form in nature. It would require a cost-effective smelting, or "reduction," process to become useful as a common metal.

The story is told that when Charles Martin Hall was just a student at Oberlin College, he was inspired by a chemistry professor's remark that "if anyone should invent a process by which aluminum could be produced on a commercial scale, not only would he be a great benefactor to the world, but would also be able to lay up for himself a great fortune." In 1886, working with simple chemicals in the woodshed adjacent to his kitchen, the twenty-two-year-old Hall invented a smelting process that remains the basis for producing aluminum to this day.

Hall soon found that few people appreciated the full significance of his discovery. His first employer, a sophisticated metallurgical firm in Cleveland, granted him neither the leeway nor the funds to commercialize his process. By 1891, however, he had moved rapidly into full-scale production after securing backing and managerial assistance from a small group of chemists and engineers in Pittsburgh. To bring the cost of the metal within reach of industrial customers, he had to produce it in large quantities, but even relatively inexpensive aluminum, at $1.21 per pound, "didn't seem to interest anyone," he wrote.

The price came down to $.36 by the turn of the century and would plunge lower still as a consequence of technological improvements and higher scale production. But it was hard work for the company that became Alcoa to develop the large-scale markets that would justify what was becoming a very "capital-intensive" business. Demand had to be cultivated as much as the technology itself. Established mills and foundries had little incentive to experiment with the metal, which required novel machining techniques. In the meantime, the company lost money, went into debt, and turned to "patient capital" in the form of substantial financial backing from the Pittsburgh bankers Andrew and Richard Mellon. Alcoa would be the first of a series of speculative long-term investments in high-technology industries for the Mellon brothers as they became, arguably, America's first great venture capitalists.

Alcoa's first chief executive, Alfred Hunt, worked tirelessly in the field demonstrating to would-be customers the superior properties of aluminum over other metals and materials. Alcoa's engineers worked closely with metal fabricators to learn how to use various alloys of the metal and to transform it into a variety of shapes and even some end products. In large part, Alcoa anticipated and stimulated demand by building its own fabrication plants for making sheet, wire, rod and bar, tubing extruded shapes, forgings, castings, powder, and paste. By 1910 aluminum was used in myriad ways: for electric cable, kitchen utensils, explosives, even some automotive and aircraft applications. On the horizon lay new uses in heavy transportation, building construction, and general engineering. Only through years of patient capital and entrepreneurial perseverance did Alcoa finally secure for its product "a position among commercial metals where it is treated entirely on its own merits . . . and is ranked among metals according to its value." Moreover, at the time of his premature death in 1911, Charles Martin Hall was history's wealthiest inventor.

Henry Ford's "lack of precedent" created opportunities in the service sector as well, for those enterprising enough to scout them out. When Arthur Lowes Dickinson was the U.S. partner of the British accounting firm Price Waterhouse around the turn of the twentieth century, the American market was vast but undeveloped. In London business came in over the transom, but in the United States Dickinson violated all sense of professional propriety by sending out some 36,000 announcements to bankers, lawyers, and merchants. Dickinson grasped what all managers of would-be multinational enterprises had to appreciate—that circumstances varied and markets were local.

> We cannot afford to sit down and wait for business to come to us as you can in England; our competitors are all much in evidence and consequently better known than we are. . . . Even assuming that we have a better reputation and do better work . . . does not go far with people like the majority of the Commercial classes here, who have very little knowledge of the subject and do not know good work from bad.
>
> ARTHUR LOWES DICKINSON

Historical Echo: The Kodak Camera and the Apple Computer

The founding of Apple Computer in the 1970s has become a legend of modern business. Two seemingly unlikely entrepreneurs, an electronic engineer named Stephen Wozniak and an iconoclastic rebel named Steve Jobs, began assembling computers in the garage of Jobs's parents. The first Apple was hardly user-friendly. It was little more than a circuit board in fact, lacking a case, keyboard, or screen—a machine only a hardcore enthusiast could love. But Jobs sensed the prospect of a much wider market for a very different kind of computer, and he drove his partner to create new, more accessible versions. In 1977 the pair launched the Apple II, which read floppy disks and displayed color graphics. And in 1984 they unveiled the Macintosh, which employed a graphical interface and a mouse (technologies Jobs had more or less lifted from Xerox's PARC laboratory).

The advent of Apple marked a fundamental transformation in the computer industry. What had been a highly arcane and massively expensive piece of back-office machinery became a consumer good and, ultimately, the platform of an information revolution.

(continues)

(continued)

Roughly a century before, Eastman's Kodak camera transformed the medium and market of photography in strikingly similar ways. George Eastman began his career much as Jobs and Wozniak did: as an enthusiastic amateur, experimenting in a makeshift lab he set up in his mother's kitchen to produce his own dry-plate emulsion. After numerous trials and errors, Eastman perfected his processes and set up a fairly successful business making and selling dry plates.

But he wasn't satisfied. Eastman remained frustrated by the limits of dry-plate photography and tantalized by a vision of an entirely different business. If he could invent a camera that was easier to make and simpler to operate, he became convinced, he could tap a vast number of consumers. So he went back to work, collaborating with several engineers to perfect first a new photography technology based on rolled film, then a camera to house the film and roller.

As Eastman progressed from the development to the marketing stage, he discovered that he was going to have to reengineer not just the camera but the consumer as well.

> When we started out with our scheme of film photography we expected that everybody that used glass plates would take up films. But we found that in order to make a large business we would have to reach the general public and create a new class of patrons.
>
> GEORGE EASTMAN

Eastman proved as resourceful a marketer as he had an engineer. He persuaded drugstore owners to include cameras in their stock. To brand the new product, he personally coined, in 1888, the trademark "Kodak"—a name, he later explained, that was short, new, impossible to mispronounce, and "does not resemble anything in the art and cannot be associated with anything in the art except the Kodak." He drove this intuitive stroke deep into the popular imagination with an ambitious mass-marketing campaign that proclaimed, "You press the button, we do the rest."

Like the Apple personal computer ninety years later, the Kodak camera utterly transformed the product, the market, the industry, and the material culture. The revolution we know best started in a garage; the one we have almost forgotten happened in a kitchen. Each, in its way, represented a bold reimagination of business possibilities. Each required a new definition of the market. Each transformed a highly specialized technology into an accessible consumer product, putting a powerful new medium of expression in the hands of a broad new population of users.

The march of improvement in any given field is always marked by periods of inactivity and then by sudden bursts of energy which revolutionize existing methods sometimes in a day.

George Eastman

Finding Money

With all the other problems of venturing new kinds of business came the daunting challenge of raising capital. Here too, doing business a century ago called for ingenuity and resourcefulness. The financial markets of the period were only just forming. Investors were accustomed to relatively small, short-term business ventures—a consignment of wheat, say, or a trading voyage to Canton.

Bold ventures needed bold capital, and entrepreneurs had to scramble nimbly to assemble the funds they needed to realize their visions.

John D. Rockefeller, for example, vividly recounted the story of "one of the most strenuous financial efforts I ever made":

> We had to raise the money to accept an offer for a large business. It required many hundreds of thousands of dollars—and in cash—securities would not answer. I received the message at about noon and had to get off on the three-o'clock train. I drove from bank to bank, asking each president or cashier, whomever I could find first, to get ready for me all the funds he could possibly lay hands on. I told them I would be back to get the money later. I rounded up all of our banks in the city [Cleveland], and made a second journey to get the money, and kept going until I secured the necessary amount. With this I was off on the three-o'clock train, and closed the transaction.
>
> JOHN D. ROCKEFELLER,
> *RANDOM REMINISCENCES OF MEN AND EVENTS,* 1909

Enterprises like Standard Oil were unprecedented, and building them strained existing financial resources to new limits.

> Capital was most difficult to secure, and it was not easy to interest conservative men in this adventurous business. Men of property were afraid of it, though in rare cases capitalists were induced to unite with us to a limited extent. If they bought our stock at all, they took a little of it now and then as an experiment, and we were painfully conscious that they often declined to buy new stock with many beautiful expressions of appreciation.

Standard Oil Stock

> The enterprise being so new and novel, on account of the fearfulness of certain holders in reference to its success, we frequently had to take stock to keep it from going begging, but we had such confidence in the fundamental value of the concern that we were willing to assume this risk.
>
> JOHN D. ROCKEFELLER,
> *RANDOM REMINISCENCES OF MEN AND EVENTS*, 1909

In my young manhood we had everything to do and nothing to do it with; we had to hew our own paths along new lines; we had little experience to go on. Capital was most difficult to get, credits were mysterious things.

John D. Rockefeller, *Random Reminiscences of Men*

Things went only a little more easily for Harvey Firestone a few decades later as he struggled to establish himself in the tire business. He started out with a patent for fastening tires to wheels, a technology superior to anything his larger competitors had. But he started out small, buying the tires themselves from those very competitors. The operating margin was razor-thin, and Firestone's business lost money through several years of painful infancy. He knew he needed to expand into tire manufacturing. The problem was getting the capital.

> I was on the hunt day and night for men to buy our stock. It was no easy matter to sell stock in a company that had no assets excepting a patent on which it was losing money. For years I never saw a man with money without turning over in my mind how I could transfer some of his money into our stock.
>
> HARVEY FIRESTONE, *MEN AND RUBBER*, 1926

Above all, Firestone wanted the backing of Will Christy, president of the Central Savings & Trust Company of Akron and "the biggest man in Akron." Christy's support, Firestone recognized, would be not only valuable financially but invaluable in lending the business the prestige to attract other investors. (Think of the situation as analogous to attracting the attention of Jim Clark in Silicon Valley today.)

> The trouble was I could not get to him. He had a big office and secretaries and all the usual safeguards of a busy man, and I could not get past those guards.
>
> HARVEY FIRESTONE, *MEN AND RUBBER*, 1926

So Firestone did some scheming that resulted in a carefully staged meeting:

"I kept tab on Will Christy's plans, and I learned that he was going to California with his wife for a vacation of several months. I found that he was going to stop over at the Auditorium Hotel in Chicago on his way out, and I took a train ahead of his to Chicago, registered at the hotel, made certain that Mr. and Mrs. Christy had registered later in the evening, and made equally certain that they did not see me that evening. . . . The next morning I was up very early and kept out of sight until I saw Mr. and Mrs. Christy going in for breakfast. Quite by accident, of course, I met them at the door of the dining room.

We had breakfast together. He inquired about our business. One thing led naturally to another, and before breakfast was over he had bought $10,000 worth of stock."

HARVEY FIRESTONE, *MEN AND RUBBER,* 1926

Never mind that Firestone would eventually change his mind about the benefits of corporate ownership and laud Ford for taking Ford Motor Company private. In order to venture, he needed venture capital, if only to get started.

So did Edison, another of Firestone's close business friends. Indeed, throughout his business career Edison devoured substantial sums of seed capital—his own and that of outside investors. He was never quite comfortable dealing with the financiers who backed him. But he could not do without them. The pattern established itself as early as 1870, when Edison set up his first substantial manufacturing operation in Newark, New Jersey, a facility to make an improved stock ticker for the Gold & Stock Telegraph Company. One of Edison's lab assistants later recalled:

"General [Marshall] Lefferts was anxious to secure from Edison the rights to the improved [stock] tickers," for he felt they should be owned by the company. One day he called the young man into his office and asked him how much he thought he should receive for them. Edison felt that five thousand dollars would be a suitable sum, but was prepared to accept as low as three thousand. Even that amount was so large that he hesitated to name it.

"Well, General, suppose you make me an offer," he replied.

"How would $40,000 suit you?"

Forty thousand dollars! The mere mention of such a staggering sum nearly caused young Edison to faint. He stammered out finally that he thought it was fair, and so it was arranged to have a contract drawn to that effect.

Three days later Edison came in to sign the documents and get the money. Even yet he could scarcely believe it was true; it seemed too unreal. So, when the general handed him a piece of paper drawn on the Bank of New York for the sum named, Edison was still unconvinced. It was the first check he had ever received and he would not believe it was true until he got the actual cash.

Ignorantly he handed it in at the bank teller's wicket without endorsing it. The teller with a smile handed it back and tried to tell Edison what was wrong. In his deafness and excitement, Edison failed to understand, and walked out of the bank in a cold sweat, ready to believe he had been cheated.

The only thing to do was to go back to the general and he did so, to tell how the check was turned back. His account of his experience caused much hilarity at the office. A clerk was sent back with him, the check was properly endorsed, and forty thousand dollars in small bills was paid over. The teller thought he would continue the joke by making the bills as small as possible, and as a result Edison had to stuff them into the pockets of his overcoat and in all his other pockets, also.

" Thus laden down with currency, he crossed the Hudson on a ferry boat and went to Newark where he sat up all night, guarding his wealth. In the morning he returned to New York and sought the aid of the general who introduced him to a bank account. "

FRANCIS JEHL, *MENLO PARK REMINISCENCES*, 1936

I kept only payroll accounts. I kept no books. I preserved a record of my own expenditures on one hook, and the bills on another hook, and generally gave notes in payment. The first intimation that a note was due was the protest; after that I had to hustle around and raise the money. This saved the humbuggery of bookkeeping, which I never understood, and besides, the protest fees were only one dollar and fifty cents.

Thomas Edison

Edison Phonograph Works Stock

The anecdote is amusing, but revealing too. In the coming years, as Edison's business ventures evolved into Edison Electric and then into General Electric, the inventor remained always uneasy dealing with his financiers. Edison sold off his General Electric stock soon after that company went public, turning to new ventures. Firestone would conclude:

> " Mr. Edison is a great inventive genius with a wide business experience; he had had a marvellous laboratory experience, but he is impatient of detail that is not connected with his experiments and really his largest interest is in development. "
>
> HARVEY FIRESTONE, *MEN AND RUBBER*, 1926

Conclusion: From Brass, New Roads

The great showman Phineas T. Barnum, who moved from one project to the next with the seemingly cheerful insouciance that many entrepreneurs display when they have more ideas than resources, once told a revealing story. He was laying plans to acquire a grand edifice to house his fabulous sideshows.

> " I met a friend one day in the street and told him my intentions. "You buy the American Museum?" he said with surprise, for he knew that my funds were at ebb-tide; "what do you intend to buy it with?"
> "Brass," I replied, "for silver and gold I have none." "
>
> P. T. BARNUM

Barnum had put his finger right on it: in the final analysis, brass was the vital currency where venturing was concerned. Figures like Henry Ford, George Eastman, and Thomas Edison did not share anything like a distinct personality type or a specific strategy of development. But they all had brass, and they all learned to parlay brass until they could get gold or silver. They had to, because products like the Model T, the Kodak camera, and aluminum required vision to be imagined as business possibilities, and commitment to be realized as business realities.

What defined the great industrialists as venturers, ultimately, was something more basic than strategies or tactics, technologies or markets. Whatever the invention, whatever the business plan, they all shared a vital willingness to look beyond the categories and boundaries they started with. They were compelled by a primal drive to create, to make something new.

Harvey Firestone felt it acutely. Here was a man who built up a business from a small factory into a corporate giant. But when, toward the end of his career, he offered advice to young businesspeople just starting out, Firestone looked beyond his rubber factories. He gazed, almost wistfully, into the new fields of enterprise that were just starting to take shape. And he urged the next generation to look even further ahead.

> The best course to-day is to go into the organization which has already accumulated capital and get a wide scope for one's ability. But there is no rule. While this is being written, probably some man with only a few dollars in his pocket is founding a business that will, within the next twenty years, run into the millions. Since I have started in business, I have seen the motion pictures and the radio grow into vast industries in the hands of men who only here and there had any capital to start with.
>
> HARVEY FIRESTONE

But then, Firestone had been intimately involved in the emergence and growth of the industry that had defined his age. He had helped drive the automobile to the center of American business, of American life, of the American dream. He had participated, in other words, in the drama that the age's most visionary entrepreneur, Thomas Edison, identified as its most important venture.

"The automobile has made better roads—but the best roads of progress it has made are not physical. They are those mystic paths which urge men into new worlds of imagination and incentive.

THOMAS EDISON

2

COMPETING

*If you have an idea, that is good. If you also have
ideas as to how to work it out, that is better.*

—HENRY FORD

The great industrialists became known as "Robber Barons" in
part because so many of them competed so ruthlessly. They
overturned an earlier, smaller, slower world of family farms and
local enterprises. And in its place they created a very different
business environment, an intense arena of barter and battle. At
first, you *could* do business in radically new ways—on a vastly expanded scale, at a sharply accelerating pace, across a widening
scope of enterprise—and then all of the sudden you *had* to. Because if you weren't keeping up, your competitors certainly were.
And they were bent on swallowing or crushing you.

The great industrialists competed ruthlessly because the
stakes of business were climbing dramatically. Enormous new
markets were opening; dazzling new technologies in transportation, telecommunications, electricity, chemicals, metallurgy, and
the mass production of consumer goods were creating vast new
entrepreneurial opportunities. Rockefeller in oil, Carnegie in
steel, Swift in packaged meats—they were all fighting for
footholds on ground that was just heaving up into view. As entre-

preneurs, they invented or opportunistically appropriated new ways of making products and markets. Then as competitors, they learned how to nurture, protect, and expand their creations.

The competition was brutal. But the most resourceful of them sensed and seized the opportunity to build new kinds of businesses that dominated their fields. In the process they redefined the tactics of business competition. They grasped and leveraged new strategies, new ways of gaining competitive advantage—strategies like economies of scale, continuous flow, mass production and mass distribution, and branding. Ultimately they built businesses that remain household names today—Procter & Gamble, General Motors, DuPont.

Mastering the Details

If today's economy runs on silicon, the economy of the Industrial Age ran and rested squarely on steel. According to the man who forged the world's largest and most competitive steel company, it was a wonderfully straightforward business, at least once it was up and running:

> The eighth wonder of the world is this: two pounds of iron-stone purchased on the shores of Lake Superior and transported to Pittsburgh; two pounds of coal mined in Connellsville and manufactured into coke and brought to Pittsburgh; one half pound of limestone mined east of the Alleghenies and brought to Pittsburgh; and these four and one half pounds of material manufactured into one pound of solid steel and sold for one cent. That's all that need be said about the steel business.
>
> ANDREW CARNEGIE

He made it sound so simple, so pure. But behind Carnegie's lyric paean lay hard-edged business savvy, honed in battle. In fact, the steel business was not simple—not in Carnegie's hands. Like all the leading industrialists of the late nineteenth century, Carnegie thrived because he mastered the details and exploited his logistics more methodically than his competitors did. Strategy was not just a general problem; it required command of the particulars of a particular enterprise. Carnegie won a decisive advantage over his rivals by controlling his costs—by breaking them down more concretely, more finely, more imaginatively.

" As I became acquainted with the manufacture of iron I was greatly surprised to find that the cost of each of the various processes was unknown. Inquiries made of the leading manufacturers of Pittsburgh proved this. It was a lump business, and until stock was taken and the books balanced at the end of the year, the manufacturers were in total ignorance of results. I heard of men who thought their business at the end of the year would show a loss and had found a profit, and vice versa. "

Symbolic depiction of Carnegie's steelmaking. From a profile of Carnegie in *The Cosmopolitan Magazine*, 1902.

I felt as if we were moles burrowing in the dark, and this to me was intolerable.

ANDREW CARNEGIE

The same instincts created decisive advantages in the burgeoning tire industry:

" Success is the sum of detail. It might perhaps be pleasing to imagine one's self beyond detail and engaged only in great things. But . . . if one attends only to great things and lets the little things pass, the great things become little—that is, the business shrinks. "

HARVEY FIRESTONE, *MEN AND RUBBER*, 1926

Cutting Out Waste

Exacting attention to accounts, to the costs of production, and to opportunities to tighten up also undergirded the rise of John D. Rockefeller in the oil business. Rockefeller prided himself on paring the pennies out of his operational costs, even to the point, it was said, of ordering his operatives to save a drop of solder on each barrel of oil. He claimed with satisfaction:

" As I began my business life as a bookkeeper, I learned to have great respect for figures and facts, no matter how small they were. "

JOHN D. ROCKEFELLER

Like the great industrialists who preceded him, Ford continuously scoured his operations. Even waste as seemingly disposable as floor sweepings could add up:

> The sweepings from our floors net us $600,000 a year. We fight waste constantly. We use gases from the blast furnaces, sawdust, shavings, coke-dust, etc. The steam power plant is thus fired almost entirely from waste products.

HENRY FORD

6

Everything but the Grunt

The drive to speed production and eliminate waste was one of the great contributions the great industrialists made to economic life. In the highly competitive processed-meat industry, for example, J. Ogden Armour conducted his Chicago-based business at a frantic pace. He kept constantly busy, knowing that he could not afford to let up. "Whoever admits that he is too busy to improve his methods," he said, "has acknowledged himself to be at the end of his rope."

Taking up disassembly techniques first employed at Cincinnati (the "Porkopolis" of the mid-1800s), Armour and his principal rival, Gustavus Swift, built up highly efficient slaughtering production lines. They honed their operations continuously, always looking for new efficiencies, new ways to move animals more quickly through the process of slaughter and packing.

They also learned how to extract and exploit the animal by-products to make oleomargarine, glue, beef extract, fertilizers, knife handles (out of shinbones), and countless other products, until Gustavus Swift could claim with scarcely a scrap of exaggeration: "Now we use all of the hog but the grunt."

The Rockefeller eyes are small and glittering, like the eyes of a rat. By the same token, the contour of the Rockefeller mouth is suggestive of the cutting, gnawing rodent teeth. Once I saw where a rat had gnawed through six inches of solid oak. Think of the patient, painful labor involved! When he got through, however, hundreds of bushels of wheat were at the mercy of that Rockefeller of a rat.

Muckraker Alfred Henry Lewis

Obsessed with getting the most production using the least movement of men and machinery, Ford eventually began moving his engines and cars past his workers, rather than the other way around. This critical bit of reengineering, partly inspired by the "disassembly" lines of the Chicago meatpackers, yielded huge savings and forged what became the emblem of the Industrial Age: the assembly line.

Every piece of work in the shops moves. Save ten steps a day for each of the 12,000 employees, and you will have saved fifty miles of wasted motion and misspent energy.

HENRY FORD

At Ford's production was improving all the time; less waste, more spotters, strawbosses, stoolpigeons (fifteen minutes for lunch, three minutes to go to the toilet, the Taylorized speedup everywhere, reach under, adjust washer, screwdown bolt, shove in cotterpin, reachunder adjustwasher, screwdown bolt, reachunderadjustscrewdownreachunderadjust until every ounce of life was sucked off into production and at night the workmen went home grey shaking husks).

John Dos Passos, *The Big Money*, 1936

Strategic Expansion

Because the men who built Carnegie Steel, Standard Oil, and Ford Motor Company bent so closely over their books, they were ready when they looked up to redraw their businesses in bold strokes. It was his meticulous accounting, Rockefeller maintained, that enabled Standard Oil to expand so swiftly, so decisively. Indeed, as he figured out that he could afford to expand, the oil tycoon rapidly decided he could not afford *not* to.

" I ascribe the success of the Standard Oil Company to its consistent policy of making the volume of its business large through the merit and cheapness of its products. It has spared no expense in utilizing the best and most efficient method of manufacture. . . . It has not hesitated to sacrifice old machinery and old plants for new and better ones. It has placed its manufactories at the points where they could supply the markets at the least expense. It has not only sought markets for its principal products, but for all possible by-products, sparing no expense in introducing them to the public in every nook and corner of the world. It has not hesitated to invest millions of dollars in methods for cheapening the gathering and distribution of oils by pipelines, special cars, tank steamers, and tank wagons. It has created tank stations at railroad centers in every part of the country to cheapen the storage and delivery of oil. It has had faith in American oil and has brought together vast sums of money for the purpose of making it what it is. "

JOHN D. ROCKEFELLER,
RANDOM REMINISCENCES OF MEN AND EVENTS, 1909

> None of us ever dreamed of the magnitude of what proved to be the later expansion. We did our day's work as we met it, looking forward to what we could see in the distance and keeping well up to our opportunities, but laying our foundations firmly.
>
> **John D. Rockefeller,**
> *Random Reminiscences of Men and Events,* 1909

Take, for example, the barrels in which Standard shipped its oil. When Rockefeller started out, he bought the barrels in which he shipped kerosene, just as Cleveland's other oil refiners did, paying $2.50 for each one. The cost grated on him, though, so he investigated and decided he could make dry, tight casks much more cheaply in-house. Standard Oil promptly bought up and expanded a cooperage of its own. Soon Rockefeller was selling barrels to his competitors.

Even the most bitter of his critics grudgingly admired the combination of meticulous accounting and strategic vision that guided Rockefeller's rise to monopoly:

> With Mr. Rockefeller's genius for detail, there went a sense of the big and vital factors in the oil business, and a daring in laying hold of them which was very like military genius. He saw strategic points like a Napoleon, and he swooped on them with the suddenness of a Napoleon. . . . The man saw what was necessary to his purpose, and he never hesitated before it. His courage was steady—and his faith in his ideas unwavering. He simply knew that was the thing to do, and he went ahead with the serenity of the man who knows.
>
> IDA TARBELL,
> *HISTORY OF THE STANDARD OIL COMPANY,* 1905

> Something in the nature of J. D. Rockefeller had to occur in America. . . . His cold persistence and ruthlessness may arouse something like horror, but for all that he was a forward-moving force, a constructive power.
>
> **H. G. Wells, *The Work, Wealth, and Happiness of Mankind,* 1932**

The Imperative of Flow

Carnegie was equally Napoleonic in his drive to expand, to acquire or build competing steel mills, as well as the blast furnaces, iron ore reserves, and coal mines he needed to ensure a steady flow of supplies to his mills.

" In 1888 we had twenty millions of dollars invested; in 1897 more than double or over forty-five millions. The 600,000 tons of pig iron we made per annum in 1888 was trebled; we made nearly 2,000,000. Our product of iron and steel was in 1888, say, 2,000 tons per day; it grew to exceed 6,000 tons. Our coke works then embraced about 5,000 ovens; they were trebled in number, and our capacity, then 6,000 tons, became 18,000 tons per day. Our Frick Coke Company in 1897 had 42,000 acres of coal land, more than two thirds of the true Connellsville vein. . . . It may be accepted as an axiom that a manufacturing concern in a growing country like ours begins to decay when it stops extending. "

ANDREW CARNEGIE, *AUTOBIOGRAPHY,* 1920

As Carnegie expanded his scale of operation, he realized growing economies of scale; he found, in other words, that he could make steel much more cheaply in bigger batches, while running his mills continuously.

> In enormous establishments . . . it costs the manufacturer much less to run at a loss per ton or per yard than to check his production. Stoppage would be serious indeed.
>
> ANDREW CARNEGIE

For businesses like Carnegie Steel and Standard Oil, preventing "stoppage" thus became a driving imperative. Carnegie had to keep feeding his mills a steady stream of iron ore, limestone, and coal in order to keep them running at peak efficiency. This was not a business for the tentative or the faint of heart. Competing effectively meant operating on an increasingly large scale, and that in turn meant doing whatever it took to secure supplies of raw material upstream.

Vertical integration, in short, became a powerful competitive tool. Few wielded it more effectively than Carnegie. As one social critic put it:

> His system was simplicity itself. He made a profit off everybody, permitted nobody to make a profit off him. He needed iron-ore, wherefore he owned iron-mines. He needed coal, wherefore he owned coal-mines. He needed coke, wherefore he owned coke-ovens. He needed money, wherefore he owned banks.
>
> ALFRED HENRY LEWIS,
> PROFILING CARNEGIE IN COSMOPOLITAN, 1908

The same logic also led the steel magnate to buy and build up a fleet of ore carriers on the Great Lakes and numerous other ancillary ventures. Thus, Carnegie started out building steel mills but ended up acquiring a business empire, with steel at its core. Ultimately, as one of his managers proudly announced, Carnegie's monumental Edgar Thomson Steel Mills became entirely self-sufficient.

> From the moment . . . crude stuffs were dug out of the earth until they flowed in a stream of liquid steel in the ladles, there was never a price, profit, or royalty paid to an outsider.
>
> JAMES H. BRIDGES

Rockefeller pruning roses. From *The Literary Digest*, May 6, 1905. Rockefeller had claimed "The American Beauty rose can be produced in all its splendor only by sacrificing the early buds that grow up around it."

Handling Rivals: Carnegie and Rockefeller

They were the two supreme competitors of the nineteenth century, and they built their businesses using strikingly similar tactics. But they brought quite different strategic instincts to bear on their competitors as they gained the upper hand.

Carnegie acquired some competing businesses but generally disposed of the people who had run them. There was no room in Carnegie Steel for "failed" rivals; the steel magnate preferred to grow his own partners and managers.

Rockefeller, on the other hand, courted his competitors. He preferred to buy out rival oil refiners and then take on the best of their managers as partners in his expanding empire. When, for instance, he got a stranglehold (temporary, as it turned out) on the railroads transporting oil from Pennsylvania to Cleveland, he made the round of Cleveland refiners and presented them with an ultimatum: join Standard Oil or be choked off.

Some refiners remembered the offer as a warning:

> There is no chance for anyone outside. But we are going to give everybody a chance to come in. You are to turn over your refinery to my appraisers, and I will give you Standard Oil Company stock or cash, as you prefer, for the value we put upon it. I advise you to take the stock. It will be for your own good.

For his own part, Rockefeller insisted that his overtures were friendly:

> We will take your burdens. We will utilize your ability; we will give you representation; we will unite together and build a substantial structure on the basis of cooperation.

(continues)

(continued)

Of course, it was Rockefeller who was setting the price. And as he insisted: "The good will of a business which is losing money is not worth much."

Whatever the tone, whatever the terms, the pitch worked powerfully on most of Cleveland's refiners. In a period of about six weeks in the early spring of 1872, Rockefeller assimilated twenty-two of his twenty-six Cleveland competitors, making Standard Oil the largest oil refiner in the world.

It was forced upon us. We had to do it in self-defense. The oil business was in confusion and daily growing worse. Someone had to make a stand.

John D. Rockefeller

In person Mr. Rockefeller is a huge-boned bulk of a man, like his father before him. He is not handsome, because he has no hair; he is not happy, because he has no stomach. Remembering how mankind in its civilization sits ever in the awful money-shadow of Standard Oil, I warn you that it is a fearsome thing to be at the mercy of one who has no stomach, that town and country residence of the soul.

Alfred Henry Lewis

First Mover Advantages:
The New Rules Take Hold

Chicago meatpackers Philip Armour and Gustavus Swift sensed similar market opportunities in their industry and seized them aggressively, expanding their distribution reach into national markets by designing refrigerated railroad cars capable of transporting frozen meat across the continent. When some railroads refused to carry the cars, fearing they would lose the more profitable business of shipping live animals, the meatpackers forced them to capitulate by playing them off against railroads that would. And when local butchers in distant towns and cities tried to boycott and break the new competition once the frozen meat arrived, the Chicago meatpackers fought back hard, wedging open the new markets by setting up their own warehouses and agents, forcing butchers to come to terms.

Swift and Armour moved swiftly and aggressively because they sensed they could not afford to hold back in their quest for market leadership. Swift was willing to spend to the hilt to secure market share on the eastern seaboard of the United States. As he told his son, whom he was already grooming to take over the business:

> Some day the other members of the industry would realize what was going on. And forthwith they would enter into competition to obtain a share of the eastern business. . . . Under these circumstances my father did the only thing thinkable. He went to any length to expand his business while he had the field to himself. . . . He borrowed every cent he could to build more refrigerator cars, to extend his plant, to establish his distributing machinery in the East. Every cent his business yielded went back into it again.
>
> LOUIS SWIFT, *YANKEE OF THE YARDS*, 1927

Or as Gustavus himself put it:

" If you're going to lose money, lose it. But don't let 'em nose you out. "

GUSTAVUS SWIFT

Amazon.com's Jeffrey Bezos could not have put it more succinctly.

Financial Control

Of course, Bezos has been blessed with patient investors. The Robber Barons could not always count on long-term market thinking from their financial backers. As a result, many of them remained deeply suspicious of corporate ownership, getting and keeping as much financial control as they could.

" Individual management will show its superiority in the future as in the past. . . . When a concern becomes the football of Wall Street, it is owned by nobody or anybody, nobody knows who—a waif that will wreck at the first storm. Some corporations there are, in which a few persons are prominent as owners and in which individual management is marked, that are exceptions to the rule; but where stock is held by a great number, what is anybody's business is nobody's business. "The eye of the owner maketh a fat horse, not the eye of the salaried official." "

ANDREW CARNEGIE

Harvey Firestone also believed corporate ownership created obstacles to long-term growth.

> " Every American business of consequence has been built up by one man staying on the job. The corporate form of organization is only a method of defining the interests of investors. It is not a form of management. And when the stockholders vigorously help in the management, the business cannot prosper. "
>
> HARVEY FIRESTONE, *MEN AND RUBBER*, 1926

Tall chimneys continued to rise at the High-land Park plant, and to pour clouds of black smoke into the sky. Henry Ford was making steel, he was building new machinery, and new structures to house it. Sixteen hours a day he was rolling out lines of new flivvers [Model Ts], one of them every twenty-five seconds now. He was buying properties, branching out into one industry after another, to give him control of raw materials and means of making parts of his cars: steel, iron ore, coal, glass, rubber, cement—in order to make one flivver he needed a world.

Upton Sinclair, *The Flivver King*, 1937

Ford: The Apogee

Henry Ford was famous for sparring with his investors. When backers balked at building a massive new manufacturing plant, Ford determinedly bought them out and took his company private. Then he built what became the apogee of vertical integration, the Ford Motor Company's sprawling River Rouge Plant.

We are constantly experimenting with every material that enters into the car. We cut most of our own lumber from our own forests. We are experimenting in the manufacture of artificial leather because we use about

> forty thousand yards of artificial leather a day. . . . The greatest development of all, however, is the River Rouge plant, which, when it is running to its full capacity, will cut deeply and in many directions into the price of everything we make. . . . This plant is located on the river on the outskirts of Detroit and the property covers six hundred and sixty-five acres—enough for future development. It has a large slip and a turning basin capable of accommodating any lake steamship.
>
> HENRY FORD

River Rouge was an industrial world unto itself, engineered so as to give Ford (both the man and his company) total control and maximum efficiency.

> We use a great deal of coal. This coal comes directly from our mines over the Detroit, Toledo and Ironton Railway, which we control. . . . Part of it goes for steam purposes. Another part goes to the by-product coke ovens which we have established. . . . The low volatile gases from the blast furnaces are piped to the power plant boilers where they are joined by the sawdust and the shavings from the body plant. . . . Immense steam turbines directly coupled with dynamos transform this power into electricity, and all of the machinery in the tractor and body plants is run by individual motors from this electricity. . . . The large-sized coke goes to the blast furnaces. There is no manual handling. We run the melted iron directly from the blast furnaces into great ladles. These ladles travel into the shops and the iron is poured directly into the moulds.
>
> HENRY FORD

Other industrialists listened and learned. Harvey Firestone, for one, deeply admired Ford's strategic instinct:

"
The lesson I learned [from Ford] was that a manufacturing operation should be carried through without a stop from the raw material to the finished product, and that no man can be said to control his business unless also he can control his sources. The larger the business, the greater are the possible economies.
"

HARVEY FIRESTONE, *MEN AND RUBBER*, 1926

The Revolution Hits Retail

Well before Henry Ford was probing the limits of scale economies in mass production, other entrepreneurs were using essentially similar competitive tactics to overhaul mass distribution. The strategy of creating and maintaining flow proved as powerful in businesses like mail-order retailing as it did in steel manufacturing and oil refining. Mail-order retailers like Montgomery Ward and Sears, Roebuck and Company quickly came to depend on churning a high, steady volume of sales through their systems in order to sell at prices far below what their smaller, scattered competitors could profitably charge.

"
In my humble opinion We Must Have Volume—whether it be Easy in the Boat or not. Our very life Demands Volume—and if one hot fire doesn't get it I would build more fires.
"

RICHARD W. SEARS

Historical Echo: Sears, P&G, and Wal-Mart

The expansion of large discount retailers at the end of the twentieth century has provoked hostility and concern for the fate of the smaller retail establishments they are putting out of business. Wal-Mart—with its huge warehouses and its efficient inventory controls—has come to symbolize not just the gutting of small-town merchants but also the more personal way of life they represented.

Not for the first time. A century before Sam Walton set off the seismic disturbances rattling the stores along Main Street, Richard Sears shook up an earlier network of rural general stores, wholesalers, and "jobbing" middlemen.

Sears was able to underprice the general stores because it dealt in huge volumes that created substantial economies of scale and commanded deep discounts from the company's suppliers. Isolated stores could not compete on price, nor could they stock anything like the vast assortment Sears offered.

But rural storekeepers struck back wherever and however they could. They organized boycotts. They hosted bonfires of Sears catalogs. They pressured local newspapers to refuse ads from the mail-order house, which they dubbed "Shears and Rawbuck" and "Rears and Soreback." The displaced merchants were trying to protect their turf. But they insisted they were also guarding more basic principles. One opponent proclaimed:

> These mammoth institutions, which employ thousands of workers, doing their business entirely through the medium of their bulky catalogs, spending no money in the community whence they derive annually millions of dollars of patronage, are forcing increasing

(continues)

(continued)

numbers of home merchants to the wall and, so their opponents claim, are "making commercial graveyards of once prosperous towns."

Sears fired back in its catalogs and in circulars to its customers.

Our business has been built up to its present size as a result of the fairest and most liberal policy known to the Mercantile World. Our millions of customers can testify to our fair, square and honest dealing. We have sold good goods at very low prices, saved money for thousands upon thousands of people, and in the process of doing this a few merchants have been compelled to ask smaller profits than they otherwise would ask, in order to try to meet our competition. . . . The merchants have brought this case, not the people. The People are our Friends.

Competition for the hinterland markets was fierce and bloody. Companies like Sears struck many Americans as deeply destructive forces, restructuring traditional commercial relationships in ways that threatened to fray the very fabric of American society. Still, Sears grew inexorably, drawing customers, dislodging competitors trying to continue to do business in old, suddenly unprofitable ways.

Producers of consumer goods also destroyed old distribution channels and their institutions, in the name of efficiency. In 1919, for example, Procter & Gamble restructured its distribution mechanism by cutting out wholesalers and shipping directly to retail outlets. Even though this move severed relationships with a series of longtime partners, P&G decided it had to be done.

"If we supplied the retailer with what he needs on a week-to-week basis, the outflow from our plants would likewise be a steady week-to-week flow. If we are to avoid periodic layoffs, the solution seems to be to sell so that we will be filling retail shelves as they are emptied. In that way, our outflow will be as steady as the retailer's. And we can stabilize our employment year-round to match the retailer's year-round sales."

WILLIAM PROCTER

Three-quarters of a century later, flow between the company and its retail distributors would tighten again when P&G and Wal-Mart set up satellite-based, real-time information systems linking factories and warehouses directly to checkout computers in stores, enabling near-seamless coordination of supply to demand. Thus, consumer goods companies—producers and retailers alike—maintained their competitive edge through episodic dredging and rechanneling of their flows of goods.

Competing in the New Markets

The great industrialists competed as intensely in the marketplace as they did in factories. Their competition fostered the emergence of mass consumerism, ushering in revolutionary new ways of selling. As they expanded their markets to national and international dimensions, entrepreneurs experimented, invented, appropriated, and adapted new ways of broadcasting themselves and their goods and services. It took vision, but it also took grit, resourcefulness, and dogged perseverance. Above all, it took an instinct for salesmanship.

"Many men who are not worth over five hundred dollars at the moment this is printed will be millionaires in less than five years. That prediction involves no risk. It will happen. Who they are, by name, I do not know. But I know what they are. They are salesmen."

WILLIAM WRIGLEY JR.

Making Chewing Gum Palatable

Wrigley had a knack for salesmanship himself. His aggressive ambition and bold marketing instinct eventually made him a major entrepreneur—once he stumbled onto the right product. The son of a soap manufacturer, he began in business by selling soap, first for his father in Philadelphia, then in Chicago, where he set up his own business in 1889. To woo dealers to his product, Wrigley gave away premiums with major orders—umbrellas, rugs, baby carriages, cuspidors, whatever seemed to draw the dealers.

Along the way he switched from soap to baking powder, still experimenting with different kinds of premium incentives. When he tried including chewing gum (still a novelty product at the time), dealers began asking if they could buy the gum without the baking powder. Sensing a new opportunity, Wrigley pounced. In 1892 he began marketing his own brand of chewing gum, in two flavors: Spearmint and Juicy Fruit. (The gum, of course, came with premiums of its own.)

Now Wrigley was off and running. He invested heavily in advertising, plastering cityscapes and railroad lines with billboards. On several occasions he went so far as to ship four sticks of gum to every person listed in phone books across America.

Call him the Steve Case of his generation, for Wrigley was determined to blanket the country with his gum as thoroughly as Case has inundated it today with free America On-Line disks.

(continues)

(continued)

Like Case, Wrigley advertised as boldly as he did because he sensed an opportunity to build something new and he recognized that doing so would require new selling methods. Once he launched his campaign he never flagged. When, for example, a sharp national depression in 1907 forced businesses to cut back on "extras" like advertising, Wrigley actually stepped up his marketing campaigns.

Advertising of all sorts had fallen off. Everywhere among manufacturers you heard reasons for not advertising, for exercising less than the ordinary selling effort. The more I thought about the attitude, the more I wondered at it. It was not only that they were not taking advantage of the ordinary opportunities. They were missing something that looked to me tremendously like an extraordinary opportunity, because so few people were advertising at that time.

WILLIAM WRIGLEY JR.

Half the money I spend on advertising is wasted, and the trouble is, I don't know which half.

Department store magnate John Wanamaker

Equally assiduous cultivation prepared the ground for another consumer product popularized during this period of business expansion: the cigarette. Going into the late nineteenth century, most Americans who consumed tobacco did so in the form of chewing tobacco or cigars, neither of which lent itself particularly well to machine production. Cigarettes, on the other hand, *could* be made in huge batches by new machines. If people could be taught to buy them. It was James Buchanan Duke who put the possibilities together.

I remember the first time young Duke came into my cigar store. He had ridden up on the steam-driven "L" which used to drop live cinders on pedestrians and horses alike. He was tall, gawky, reddish, with a Southern accent thick as butter. He wanted to sell me some of his newfangled machine-made cigarettes on consignment. I told him I wouldn't handle cigarettes under any circumstances; that my customers didn't want 'em. Besides, the only name I knew of down this way was Bull Durham. He didn't seem to mind much. Within a few months the trade paper said he'd opened a loft factory on Rivington Street. Then the billboards began to flare out with Duke ads and the newspapers too. I got circulars offering camp chairs and clocks and crayon drawings if I'd order so many thousand Duke cigarettes. Customers started asking for the cigarettes by name. The climax came when Duke began putting into each package a picture of a famous actress or athlete or the flags of all nations. That was a million-dollar idea, for the pictures came in numbered sets and the kids began pestering their dads for them. Soon collecting pictures became a craze and we had to order the cigarettes in quantity. As I look back on it now I think this one stunt, more than any other, really put the cigarette over with the public.

NEW YORK MERCHANT ASA LEMLEIN

Duke's aggressive marketing instinct would create a vast new industry—and of course a consuming habit (literally) that has become an enduring public health problem.

Finding the Pitch

The success of the American Museum, according to its founder, was due to a kind of advertising that was designed

> to arrest public attention; to startle, to make people talk and wonder; in short, to let the world know that I had a museum.
>
> P. T. BARNUM

True to form, Barnum's advertising—whether boosting an impossibly old woman, a fantastic mermaid, or a child masquerading as a midget—was an extension of his showmanship. A bit like the promoters of professional wrestling today, he was a master tongue-in-cheek showman, and something of a psychologist as well. Altogether he possessed, in spades, what he listed as the vital components that made up a salesman:

> A decided taste for catering to the public; prominent perceptive facilities; tact; a thorough knowledge of human nature; great suavity; and plenty of "soft soap."
>
> P. T. BARNUM

Barnumian brashness helped lodge all kinds of new products in the popular imagination. But then, many businesspeople found that a basic awareness of customers, however distant or scattered they were becoming, was the most important ingredient in selling in the new, national markets. This explains why Gustavus F. Swift patrolled his stockyards on a pony.

> When father first came to Chicago, everyone used to laugh at his habit of riding a low Texas pony which left his legs dangling almost to the ground. He would ride around on his low-slung steed buying his cattle and caring little what anyone else might think. He knew why he was doing it and he knew he was right.

In the first place, he could let himself into a cattle pen without bothering to get off his horse—or without taking a boy around with him to do this job. But more important still, he was down at the level of the cattle's backs. He could reach over and feel the butts of the cattle to see whether there was any fat there. A great many wise jokes were made about this habit of his.

Finally, however, someone inquired just why he felt the rump of every beef animal he bought. "Back where I ship these cattle to, they're bought that way. That's how I sell 'em, and how I buy 'em." He was simply applying at Chicago the test which he knew each animal would have to meet when it reached Brighton or Albany.

LOUIS SWIFT, *YANKEE OF THE YARDS*, 1927

One thing Swift insisted on was absolute honesty.

Time and again he came to my desk or called me to his and pointed out some slip-up in shipping dates, or a let-down in quality, or something else which had the appearance of a sharp corner having been cut to get an advantage for Swift and Company. He would lecture me on the specific mistake. But always he would end up by talking about the need for being honest. "We want character to go with our goods. And 16 ounces is a Swift pound."

LOUIS SWIFT, *YANKEE OF THE YARDS*, 1927

Similarly in the tire business, Harvey Firestone eventually adopted a marketing strategy that eschewed the high-profile hard sell for simple dedication to quality. He was one of Ford's most important suppliers, and he sounded more than a little like Ford when he extolled his brand of selling:

There is a great waste in selling and especially in "hurrah" selling with conventions, campaigns, contests, and all the odds and ends of high-pressure stuff that has been devised. I have tried all of it and I know. The place to start selling is in the factory, and if the articles we make are not good enough consistently to be sold to the public without any hypnotic processes, then they are not good enough to sell at all.

HARVEY FIRESTONE, *MEN AND RUBBER*, 1926

The Brand as a Competitive Weapon

Whatever their methods or philosophies, salesmen like Wrigley, Swift, and Firestone were all scrambling to build their brands. As the contours of national markets emerged, entrepreneurs had to learn how to create distinct consumer perceptions of their products and their businesses. Figure out how to do that, and the possibilities were boundless. John Pemberton sensed it. When the Atlanta druggist concocted a dark sugar water, he knew he had a potentially huge product on his hands. But how to get it into consumers' hands?

If I could get $25,000, I would spend $24,000 advertising, the remainder in making Coca-Cola. Then we would all be rich.

JOHN PEMBERTON

He couldn't. But Pemberton was right, and when Asa Candler, who bought the rights to Pemberton's formula, began advertising Coca-Cola, he began building it into what would arguably become the world's best-known product, an icon of the global marketplace.

It was a new kind of problem, a new set of skills to work up, a new way to compete. Mastering it became the basis of business for firms like the Cincinnati soap and candle manufacturer Procter & Gamble.

P&G initially built its reputation among a loose network of distant storekeepers by dint of scrupulously fair dealing and by living up to a principle its founder, James Gamble, had once recorded in his diary:

> When you cannot make pure goods and full weight, go to something else that is honest, even if it is breaking stone.

JAMES GAMBLE

P&G's approach to advertising was carefully cloaked in the appearance of respectability, steering a course between the hard sell of Wrigley's gum and the soft soap of Barnum's illusions. Though crafted to entice through the evocation of good feelings, its advertising was always literally true.

"It Floats"

P&G was a pioneer in crafting a trademark—the famous crescent moon and thirteen stars—to identify its products.

Initially the trademark identified the firm's products to shippers and retailers. But over time Procter & Gamble learned to apply similar techniques to attracting or reassuring its ultimate customer, the consumer. It achieved a breakthrough in 1878 when it introduced a new white soap (employing a formula the company had bought up from a competitor). P&G lore has it that a careless workman left a batch in the mixing machine too long, injecting extra air into the soap, and the firm discovered that it was on to something only a short time later when it began getting requests from distributors for "the soap that floats."

The product may have floated to the surface as much by accident as design, but Procter & Gamble kept it there by dint of assiduous and creative effort. It rechristened the soap Ivory, drawing on Psalms 45:8—"All thy garments smell of myrrh and aloes and cassia, out of the ivory palaces whereby they have made thee glad"—and tagged it with the slogan "It floats." But the firm hit on the perfect pitch a few years later (under the marketing skills of Harley Procter) when it proclaimed that an independent chemical analysis had determined that impurities in the soap amounted to only a fraction of 1 percent.

"The Ivory . . . is 99 and 44/100 percent pure." Just why that should make Ivory a better cleanser was not clear, but it worked.

Adapting to Market Shifts

Tactics like those crafted by Procter & Gamble gradually created decisive competitive edges in consumer industries like soap and chewing gum. By the early twentieth century, they were beginning to shape the automobile industry as it took center stage in the American economy. Before Ford engineered the Model T, automakers assumed they were in a luxury market, producing a few hundred or a few thousand cars for the well-to-do. But Ford's Model T, simple, reliable, durable, and easy to repair, created a consumer revolution in the market for automobiles. He assembled the Model T, Ford later recounted, by standing the usual engineering mentality on its head: he engineered backward—not from the product but from the demand side of the business.

> We start with [the] consumer, work back through the design, and finally arrive at manufacturing. The manufacturing becomes a means to the end of service. . . . Our policy is to reduce the price, extend the operations, and improve the article. You will notice that the reduction of price comes first. We have never considered any costs as fixed. Therefore we first reduce the price to a point where we believe more sales will result. Then we go ahead and try to make the price. We do not bother about the costs. The new price forces the costs down. . . . The low price makes everybody dig for profits. We make more discoveries concerning manufacturing and selling under this forced method than by any method of leisurely investigation.
>
> HENRY FORD

Ford's dogged work steadily simplified the process of manufacturing the Model T, and he did indeed manage to bring costs down far below what his competitors assumed possible. But it was his major rival, Alfred Sloan of General Motors Corporation, who took this idea to its logical conclusion. While Henry Ford continued to crank out his basic black Model Ts in the 1920s, when per capita incomes and consumption of household goods were rising rapidly, Sloan introduced a line of automobiles for every pocketbook and every taste, in many colors and with frequent style changes. This strategy of market segmentation, along with such innovations as installment selling, used-car trade-ins, and closed auto bodies, propelled GM way past Ford as the market leader in American auto production.

> We had no stake in the old ways of the automobile business; for us change meant opportunity. . . . Mr. Ford, who had so many brilliant ideas in earlier years, seemed never to understand how completely the market had changed.
>
> ALFRED SLOAN

In this way, even great entrepreneurs are punished by change if they do not continuously adapt their strategies to it. As Sloan said: "Any rigidity . . . is severely penalized in the market."

3

MANAGING

*Enormous organizations, instead of crushing the
personal, have made it stronger, recognized it,
stimulated it, advertised it, banked on it, rewarded
it.*

—A. MONTGOMERY WARD

Creating a great business was one thing; sustaining it another. The
chain of events that moved materials into and through Carnegie's
Edgar Thomson Steel Mills, Ford's River Rouge plant, or Sears's
massive mail-order system had to be intricately coordinated and
expertly administered. Constructing managerial—dare we say *bureaucratic*—systems to run these complex business operations
was the most difficult problem the great industrialists had to
solve. They had no conventions to guide them, no recourse to
modern management theories, few precedents, and little experience. They had to invent modern management.

Managerial bureaucracies proved essential because they har-
nessed entrepreneurial energy and reduced it to reliable routine.
They enabled specialization and coordination of a multitude of
tasks, across time and space in accordance with standardized
procedures. This, in turn, improved the reliability, quality, and
speed of production. In other words, bureaucracy was efficient, at
least if it worked in the rational way it was supposed to.

Paradoxically, though, bureaucracy too had to change from time to time to remain effective. Every day a company was in business it had an opportunity to fail—to lose market share, to suffer declines in profits, to stagnate. Managing was a dynamic art, requiring constant adaptation to technological changes, market opportunities, and competitive threats. Organizational renewal was an entrepreneurial art in itself. Creators had to become, or give way to, bureaucrats. But bureaucrats had to remain creative.

Beyond the Big Boss

The force of a particular personality—a Rockefeller or a Carnegie—might launch a venture. But as both men readily admitted, they could not carry it forward without a strong reserve of administrative and technical talent.

> I have often said that this matchless organization was worth more than our works. If I had to choose upon entering manufacturing anew between "the Works" and my partners, these being without a dollar of Capital, I should let all the works go & hang on to the boys and to our unrivalled workingmen.
>
> ANDREW CARNEGIE

Thought, not money, is the real business capital.
Harvey Firestone

That was a striking claim on Carnegie's part, considering the scale of capital investment standing in the company's towering steel mills. But John D. Rockefeller echoed the endorsement.

> If, in place of these directors, the business were taken over and run by anyone but experts, I would sell my interest for any price I could get. To succeed in a business requires the best and most earnest men to manage it, and the best men rise to the top.
>
> JOHN D. ROCKEFELLER

Like Carnegie, Rockefeller recognized the crucial importance of what a later generation of entrepreneurs would term human capital. And his rivals did too. Testifying in 1879 about the Standard Oil organization, which had recently outbid him for a pipeline company, William H. Vanderbilt acknowledged that his rival's superior organization gave him a critical edge:

> There is no question about it but these men are smarter than I am a great deal. . . . I never came in contact with any class of men as smart and alert as they are in their business. They would never have got into the position they now are. And one man could hardly have been able to do it; it is a combination of men.
>
> WILLIAM H. VANDERBILT

Good business administration was, in short, an effective combination of specialized expertise. Rockefeller and Carnegie, the consummate organizers of the late nineteenth century, saw their businesses as vital collections of ideas and human potential and worked to recognize and develop talent from within. In Rockefeller's mind, the principle was closely linked with his commitment to keeping a tight strategic focus:

> We devoted ourselves exclusively to the oil business and its products. The company never went into outside ventures, but kept to the enormous task of perfecting its own organization. We educated our own men; we trained many of them from boyhood; we strove to keep them loyal by providing them full scope for their ability; they were given opportunities to buy stock, and the company itself helped them to finance their purchases.
>
> JOHN D. ROCKEFELLER

Carnegie felt much the same way. In 1896 he gave these instructions to Henry Clay Frick, his managing partner:

> Every year should be marked by the promotion of one or more of our young men. It is a very good plan to have all your heads of departments interested. . . . We cannot have too many of the right sort interested in profits.
>
> ANDREW CARNEGIE

Hire or promote from within? All things being equal, breeding up expertise in a highly technical business made sense, and Carnegie disdained those, such as J. P. Morgan, who had a penchant for hiring outsiders and paying liberally.

> Mr. Morgan buys his partners. I raise my own.
>
> ANDREW CARNEGIE

But Morgan was dealing in the rarefied precincts of high finance and had to seek out the best talent wherever he could find it. The key was to hire and promote the best. Morgan's profoundly meritocratic instincts reflected extraordinarily high standards. In 1875, while searching for a new partner to help conduct his expanding business, he wrote to his father complaining about how few people seemed "exceptional in character, ability, and experience."

> " The longer I live the more apparent becomes to me the absence of brains—particularly evenly balanced brains. "
>
> J. P. MORGAN

Morgan finally found the brains he was looking for in Egisto Fabbri, an Italian immigrant and former shipping merchant. In defiance of the social norms of blue-blooded Yankee banking, Morgan hired this "foreigner." Morgan continued to recruit only the best and the brightest and rewarded them accordingly. By World War I, his firm was poised to surpass the once preeminent European House of Rothschild as the leading transatlantic investment bank, precisely because the Rothschilds, more traditional in their mistrust of "outsiders," had been reluctant to promote anyone but family members to their partnership.

Morgan Hires a Partner

George W. Perkins was a young and fast-rising executive of the New York Life Insurance Company when he called on J. P. Morgan in 1900 to raise $125,000 for a public project in which he was interested. Morgan, who had been following Perkins's career, said to his visitor that he would pledge the full amount "if you will do something for me."

"Do something for you," said Perkins. "What?"

"Take that desk over there," Morgan said, pointing.

Perkins explained that he already had "a pretty good desk up at New York Life."

But Morgan waived him off with his characteristic bluntness and said, "No. . . . Come into the firm. . . . Let me know tomorrow if you can."

So intent was Morgan on bringing Perkins in that he not only compensated him well but allowed him to keep his position at New York Life. (Notions of conflicts of interest were not so highly developed then as now.)

The Railroads and the Rise of
Business Bureaucracy

Modern managerial organizations first took form in the railroads. They were the first businesses to become truly large, and thus to present general managers with the problems of managing things they could not see. As the general manager of the Erie Railroad explained in the 1850s:

> A Superintendent [general manager] of a line fifty miles in length can give its business his personal attention, and may be almost constantly upon the line engaged in the direction of its details; each employee is familiarly known to him, and all questions in relation to its business are at once presented and acted upon; and any system, however imperfect, may under such circumstances prove comparatively successful. In the government of a road five hundred miles in length a very different state of things exists.
>
> DANIEL C. MCCALLUM

As they scaled up, railroad operations required detailed coordination of routing, scheduling, and pricing. They required enormous amounts of capital—hence financial expertise. Bureaucratic expertise was also developed to oversee such disparate activities as purchasing; real estate management; safety; accounting; maintenance of track, bridges, and rolling stock; and a variety of specialized engineering functions. Everything had to be coordinated systematically across great distances on a continuous basis.

No wonder, then, that it is in the railroads where we first find the development of rigorous cost accounting, thick manuals of standard operating procedures, and organization charts detailing reporting relationships. Even so, it took a long time for railroad magnates to appreciate that systematic administration would enable them to manage efficiently a consolidation of competing or connecting main lines and feeder lines across vast territories. Both pressures of competition and the logic of scale economies seemed to demand it. In 1878 the superintendent of the Burlington, Quincy, and Chicago Railroad voiced the opinion of many railroad managers:

> Sooner or later the railroads of this country [will] group themselves into systems and . . . each system [will] be self-sustaining.
>
> CHARLES PERKINS

Yet railroad board directors held back. Only after the financial speculator Jay Gould forced the issue by launching sudden speculative purchases of the stock of strategic connecting lines did the larger railroads defend themselves by consolidating. Managerial bureaucracy, they discovered, could prove equal to the task of managing big systems efficiently.

The railroads became the schools of modern management. Their administrative principles could be transferred effectively to the telecommunications and electrical power industries as well as to large manufacturing and service companies. Already by the turn of the twentieth century most of the country's large companies were experimenting with ways of organizing and managing their growing corporate empires.

Bureaucracy as Stagnation

" If you analyze too carefully, you may analyze yourself out of business. "

RICHARD SEARS

Bureaucracy is more commonly known for its vices than its virtues. Its very rationality makes it suspect. Ideally, it is impersonal, dependent on no one individual, devoid of emotion. These attributes make bureaucracy efficient—up to a point. But of course, it is the nature of bureaucracy to value routine over change and procedure over initiative. All too easily it becomes subject to mindless duties and processes, immersed in red tape, rigid. It can take on a life of its own. The great industrialists, no less than the entrepreneurs of postindustrialism, struggled against the tendency.

Historical Echo:
Corporate Raiders and Efficiency

Jay Gould was a chronic, often unscrupulous, nuisance to conservative railroad owners and directors. He succeeded in gaining control of some lines, though he never developed the administrative capacity to manage them efficiently. Even so, his raids on railroad properties generally forced the industry as a whole to become more efficient. He was vilified, as corporate "raiders" tend to be, by a chorus of contemporary managers, straitlaced financiers, and muckraking journalists. Joseph Pulitzer called Gould "one of the most sinister figures that have ever flitted batlike across the vision of the American people." Others called him "the worst man on earth," "a despicable worm," and "Mephistopheles."

Consider the corporate raiders of the late 1970s and 1980s—speculators like T. Boone Pickens, Carl Icahn, and Sir James Goldsmith—who struck fear in the hearts of the leaders of "underperforming" (read poorly managed) companies. Their largely debt-financed attacks on the stock of such companies, more often than not, fell short of full-fledged takeovers. They often settled for "greenmail," or a simple run-up in their share prices, as managers countered with their own higher offers for company stock. By loading themselves up with debt, many companies were forced to do what the raiders might have done to them—sell off unnecessary assets, streamline operations, and lay off redundant managers and employees.

As Carl Icahn put it, speculative raids can be just the cure for the disease of inefficiency. Even so, late-twentieth-century takeover specialists were just about as despised as their nineteenth-century ancestors. Managers, labor leaders, and journalists criticized them for their "greed." Legislators passed laws making it harder to succeed with "unfriendly" takeovers. There was still no honor for speculative raiders, no matter how much they compelled managers to manage better.

Harvey Firestone, who stumbled, for a time, in making the transition from entrepreneur to manager, would later recall with chagrin how he became mired in bureaucratic routine.

> Gradually, I contracted the chart fever. . . . Gradually, we got an organization—a real organization, second to none in its division of duties. It seems—now that it is all over—that we never faced a duty without dividing it. . . . And then, inevitably, the men began to write letters to one another. I know of no better way of fooling oneself than writing interoffice communications and asking for reports. A man can keep himself busy that way all day long and completely satisfy his conscience that he is doing something worth while.
>
> HARVEY FIRESTONE

The result:

> I let the business get away from me in the easiest of all fashions—by thinking of an organization as something of itself instead of as a means of getting work done quickly and well.
>
> HARVEY FIRESTONE

The great problem with the organization he built up, as Firestone saw it, was that it stifled thinking and distracted his managers.

> A man may keep very busy indeed without doing any thinking at all, and the easy course—the course of least resistance—is to keep so busy that there will be no time left over for thought. Almost every man tries to dodge thought or to find a substitute for it. We try to buy thoughts ready made and guaranteed to fit, in the shape of systems installed by experts. We try to substitute discussion for thought by organizing committees; a committee may function very well indeed as

a clearing house for thoughts, but more commonly a committee organization is just an elaborate means of fooling one's self into believing that a spell spent in talking is the same as a spell spent in thinking.

HARVEY FIRESTONE

Then as now, moreover, office politics and turf battles could erupt, obscuring corporate objectives and sacrificing problem-solving to fault-finding. Edwin Fickes, the chief engineer of Alcoa, observed the emergence of interfunctional bickering within the company early in the twentieth century. When quality control became a corporatewide problem, managers in one department blamed another, who blamed another, and so on.

Passing the Buck at Alcoa

I had noted great and variable differences in output per unit, in the quality of metal produced in different works, and in the same works at different times; there were even greater opinions and theories as to the causes. There was no consensus of opinion about the causes of the trouble . . . , and as time went on, fabricating plant men became convinced that the reduction [smelting] plant operators were indifferent to their complaints, or worse; the reduction plant heads were convinced not only that [the refiners at East St. Louis were at fault], but . . . East St. Louis held that the reduction plant superintendents didn't know good ore from bad, and that their troubles certainly were due to something else, probably their own folly. Nor was East St. Louis satisfied with its bauxite; [the bauxite management] was sure that if folks from East St. Louis really would devote their undoubted energy and ability to making alumina, instead of finding fault with bauxite, great profit would accrue to the stockholders. . . . The habit of buck-passing and the writing of acrid and somewhat useless correspondence . . . was a growing evil.

Edwin Fickes

> Very few things are ever taken under "official consideration" until long after the time when they actually ought to have been done. The buck is passed to and fro and all responsibility is dodged by individuals—following the lazy notion that two heads are better than one.

Bureaucracy as Information System

It is always hard to make the case for bureaucracy. Advocates invariably sound cumbersome, overly precise, careful—like bureaucrats, naturally. Still, bureaucracy of some sort eventually became essential to doing business competitively.

Consider the experience of working with William Wrigley Jr., the gum manufacturer. Visitors dealing with Wrigley typically suffered constant interruptions as employees ducked their heads into the boss's office with questions or reports. When one visitor grew frustrated, Wrigley gently scolded him with some managerial advice:

> When these people come in here, they aren't doing it to interrupt you. They're carrying on this business. If they hear a word or two of our conversation, that's all right. I have no secrets. We're all here to make this business go, and for no other reason. Every time a man walks in or out, I've made some more money.
>
> WILLIAM WRIGLEY JR.

Wrigley was right, of course. Along with his extraordinary energy and close attention to detail, his accessibility was a big part of his company's success. But making chewing gum was one thing, running a major chemical company or an automobile company another. One chief executive can absorb only so much information and act responsibly on it.

What Wrigley did understand was that running a business was all about managing information. Bureaucracies were (and are) nothing more, or less, than *information systems*. Their value lay in how well they facilitated a sharing of knowledge. As the founder of Eastman Kodak put it,

> " The ideal large corporation is the one that makes the best use of the brains within it. "
>
> GEORGE EASTMAN

Managerial Chemistry at DuPont

Kodak did an admirable job of making the best use of its brains. But the most masterful knowledge managers of the era were the du Ponts and the people who worked with and for them in the first decades of the twentieth century. These were the pioneers who over the 1910s and 1920s reorganized DuPont and General Motors (which they came to control financially), laying in the structures—the bureaucracies—that became the most powerful knowledge systems of the early-twentieth-century business world.

Thus, within the headquarters of E. I. du Pont de Nemours Powder Company the realization took hold:

> The most efficient results are obtained at least expense when we coordinate related effort and segregate unrelated effort.

In other words, specific functions were to be placed under distinct administrative units, or departments. Expertise had to be leveraged, and information clutter cleared away. As a key first step, department heads needed full authority to make decisions:

> The principle of individual responsibility and undivided authority has been recognized [so that] the best available individual, who as head of that department is held responsible for results, and he can in his official capacity arrange every detail . . . according to his best judgment, subject only to the alternative of having someone replace him if his official judgment is not good.

In other words, managers on the lines were given the opportunity, and the responsibility, of "owning" their businesses and running them as mini-enterprises. This critical innovation unshackled DuPont from the constraints of centralized chains of command. In 1921 headquarters decreed:

> The head of each [business] will have full authority and responsibility for the operation of his industry, subject only to the authority [of a corporate executive oversight group]. He will have under him men who will exercise all the line functions necessary for a complete industry, including routine and special purchasing, manufacture, sales [and so on].

And then, crucially, the company committed itself to bringing in new blood from time to time. As one executive vice president at DuPont advised in 1919:

> " I believe that one reason the Company has been so successful is that for over twenty years the conduct of its [business] is in the hands of young men and this has served to keep off the dry rot of conservatism that sometimes accompanys [*sic*] too unchanging management. On the other hand we have sometimes lost by not getting full value out of experienced men. "
>
> HENRY HASKELL

Ford Versus General Motors: The Vindication of Bureaucracy

The epic battle between Ford and General Motors during the 1920s dramatically demonstrated the paradox of business creativity within business bureaucracy.

Our natural sympathy gravitates toward the pithy iconoclasts, who could indict organizational life with a sound bite. We nod with Henry Ford as he excoriates the organization man.

> That which one has to fight hardest against in bringing together a large number of people to do work is excess organization and consequent red tape. To my

mind there is no bent of mind more dangerous than that which is sometimes described as the "genius for organization." This usually results in the birth of a great big chart showing, after the fashion of a family tree, how authority ramifies. The tree is heavy with nice round berries, each of which bears the name of a man or of an office. Each man has a title and certain duties which are strictly limited by the circumference of his berry.

HENRY FORD

Business bureaucracies, Ford argued, were cumbersome, slow to reach decisions, and fatally cautious:

If a straw boss wants to say something to the general superintendent, his message has to go through the subforeman, the foreman, the department head, and all the assistant superintendents, before, in the course of time, it reaches the general superintendent. Probably by that time what he wanted to talk about is already history. It takes about six weeks for the message of a man living in a berry on the lower left-hand corner of the chart to reach the president or chairman of the board.

HENRY FORD, *MY LIFE AND WORK*, 1922

It makes for fun reading. But also for terrible business. Henry Ford never got his corporation organized, and he came dangerously close to running his business into the ground. An autocratic personality, he could not hold on to his best managerial talent. Nor could he generate value for his minority shareholders during the Depression, when GM was turning a profit. Perhaps no one was better than Ford at making cars. But when it came to building an organization, Ford was no match for Alfred Sloan.

Sloan on Management

Before the Whiz Kids, before Jack Welch, before the consulting gurus, there was Alfred Sloan, the strategic genius of General Motors and the consummate organization man. Sloan was a bureaucrat with the heart of an entrepreneur. He came to GM by way of MIT and the Hyatt Roller Bearing Company, which William "Billy" Durant acquired in the flurry of strategic moves that first gathered together the various automobile and automobile parts companies that became General Motors.

Sloan's view of Durant, a visionary venturer but an unsystematic corporate manager, is revealing:

> I was constantly amazed by his daring way of making decisions. My business experience had convinced me facts are precious things, to be eagerly sought and treated with respect. But Mr. Durant would proceed on a course of action guided solely, as far as I could tell, by some intuitive flash of brilliance. He never felt obliged to make an engineering hunt for facts.
>
> ALFRED SLOAN

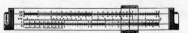

GM Before Sloan

It was quickly made plain that General Motors was a "one-man" institution. Durant was its general and he was his own colonel, his own major and his own lieutenant. He dominated it from top to bottom and brooked no interference. He is a prodigious worker and the wonder is how he attended to so many details, great and small, and lived through it all. He kept one eye on his factories and another on the stock ticker, and the while he dreamed of world conquests.

Motor World profile of William Durant, 1910

Sloan, on the other hand, had a passion for facts and did nothing impulsively. When Durant lost control over this disorganized empire and the du Ponts put Sloan in charge, the new executive immediately began equipping the company for continual, collective strategic analysis. In short, he began rewiring the firm's information systems.

He has a long, thin, tired face and a long, thin, nervous body. Mr. Sloan lacks entirely the arrogance of office. . . . General Motors is not greased to the Napoleonic individualism of Fox Film or Ford Motor. It is indeed organized specifically against the man-on-horseback idea. . . . The danger of such an organization is a lack of unified progress. The guard against this danger is Mr. Sloan, adjuster of difficulties, reconciler of temperaments, sponsor of progress.

Fortune profile of Alfred Sloan, 1930

Things came to a head in 1924. The year before, in a booming market for automobiles, GM's various car divisions geared up for major production expansions. Sloan remained apprehensive, however. Data from Donaldson Brown, a senior financial executive on loan from DuPont, indicated that sales would fall off again in 1924.

> " Mr. Brown's figures indicated that all was not well, and although I was impressed by them I hesitated to over-rule the divisional people who had the responsibility of selling. There will always be some conflict between the figure men and the salesmen, since the salesmen naturally think they can do something about a statistical situation, as they often can. "
>
> ALFRED SLOAN, *MY YEARS WITH GENERAL MOTORS*, 1964

Uneasily, then, Sloan ordered only modest scalebacks in production. But events proved the bean counters right.

> " In May 1924 Mr. Brown and I made a trip into the field to discuss distribution problems with the dealers in their places of business, and on that trip I came to know beyond doubt that the March cutbacks had been inadequate and that overproduction was not just a possibility for July but already a certainty. It is not often that the chief executive of a large corporation himself discovers visible overproduction by a physical check of the inventory. But automobiles are big units easy to count. In St. Louis, my first stop, in Kansas City, and again in Los Angeles, I stood in the dealers' lots and saw the inventories parked in rows. The figure man in this instance was right and the salesmen were wrong. "
>
> ALFRED SLOAN, *MY YEARS WITH GENERAL MOTORS*, 1964

In the wake of this setback, GM learned how to route a steady stream of sales reports from dealers through the car divisions up to headquarters. And headquarters, in turn, learned to read that data, to forecast demand, and to coordinate the purchasing of parts and supplies and the scheduling of production accordingly. The company learned, in sum, how to make its organization function as a knowledge system.

Sloan reorganized in an effort to channel information more reliably through the company. He also reorganized to impose fiscal discipline and leverage financial resources. One of the problems he encountered upon taking over management of GM was the extreme fiscal autonomy enjoyed and jealously guarded by its various divisions. The company's various car-assembly and auto-parts divisions controlled their own accounts and cash surpluses. They related to each other, he wrote, on "a horse-trading basis." There was no rational way for allocating financial resources to their best uses.

> We had no effective procedure for getting cash from the points where we happened to have some to the points where we happened to need some. I remember that Buick, for example, at that time was very loath to give up cash. This profitable division was, of course, the most prolific source of cash for the corporation, and long experience had made Buick's financial staff highly adept at delaying its report of the cash they had on hand. . . . When the corporation needed cash, the treasurer, Meyer Prentis, would try to guess how much Buick actually had and how much of it he could probably get from them. Then he would go to Flint, discuss whatever other questions might be outstanding between Buick and headquarters, and at last casually bring up the subject of cash. Buick's financial people would invariably express surprise at the size of Mr. Prentis' request and occasionally would try to resist the transfer of such a large amount.
>
> ALFRED SLOAN, *MY YEARS WITH GENERAL MOTORS*, 1964

What Sloan was trying to do was to equip GM's control systems to enable the kind of decentralized management that the company needed to produce different products for different markets. The flow of accurate information to headquarters, Sloan reasoned, enabled corporate executives to monitor the divisions through steady streams of data, rather than sporadic, frantic intervention in day-to-day management.

The key was to make the organization *more,* not less, supple. For as Sloan knew:

> Any rigidity . . . is severely penalized in the market—as we have seen was the case with Mr. Ford in the 1920s.
>
> ALFRED SLOAN, *MY YEARS WITH GENERAL MOTORS,* 1964

Ultimately it all hinged, Sloan believed, on a delicate balance between centralization and decentralization:

> The language of organization has always suffered some want of words to express the true facts and circumstances of human interaction. One usually asserts one aspect or another of it at different times, such as the absolute independence of the part, and again the need for co-ordination, and again the concept of the whole with a guiding center. Interaction, however, is the thing.
>
> ALFRED SLOAN, *MY YEARS WITH GENERAL MOTORS,* 1964

To nurture this kind of interaction, Sloan crisscrossed GM's massive organization with committees, or "policy groups," devoted to different functions, on which senior management intermingled with specialized functionaries. Rather than paralyze the corporation with endless meetings, the committees functioned with remarkable effectiveness. They took their lead from Sloan himself. The CEO recognized that working by way of committee sometimes slowed business down, but he upheld the method regardless.

> Group decisions do not come easily. There is a strong temptation for the leading officers to make decisions themselves without the sometimes onerous process of discussion, which involves selling your ideas to others.
>
> ALFRED SLOAN, *MY YEARS WITH GENERAL MOTORS,* 1964

The result at GM, at least according to *Fortune,* was something remarkable:

> [GM] has escaped the fate of those many families of vertebrates whose bodies grew constantly larger while their brain cavities grew relatively smaller. . . . It has escaped because Mr. Sloan has contrived to provide it with a composite brain commensurate with its size. His achievement may be summed up as one of inter-communication, getting all the facts before all people concerned. In essence, it is the democratic method applied to management, with the committee taking the place of a deliberative assembly. . . . To put it another way, Mr. Sloan . . . has . . . set up a Federal system, in which each state or division has a large degree of autonomy, only certain powers being reserved to the central government.

Finally, Sloan never let himself or his company believe that any given structure, any particular bureaucratic solution, was set in stone. The corporation had to continually monitor, tinker, and occasionally overhaul its organization, Sloan was convinced, to preserve the vitality of its administrative systems.

> Much of my life in General Motors was devoted to the development, organization, and periodic reorganization of . . . central management. This was required because of the paramount importance . . . of providing the right framework for decisions. There is a natural tendency to erode that framework unless it is consciously maintained.
>
> ALFRED SLOAN, *MY YEARS WITH GENERAL MOTORS,* 1964

4

LEADING

In the old days, I used to pick my own men. We all knew one another. We did not need any rules. . . . We just worked together.

We had only 12 employees in 1902. . . . Not until 1910 did we reach 1,000. Seven years later we passed 10,000, and in 1920 reached a peak of 19,800. . . . In 1902, we did a business of $150,000. In 1920, we did a business of $115,000,000, but I can say with great earnestness that financing this tremendous growth was not nearly as difficult as solving the human equation, or, to be more accurate, getting something in the nature of a comprehension of the human equation.

—Harvey Firestone, *Men and Rubber*, 1926

The ineffable quality of leadership is essential to long-term entrepreneurial success. For the great entrepreneurs of the Industrial Age, it proved vital to raising large sums of other people's money, to attracting and inspiring good managers, and to building businesses big enough and resourceful enough to survive in the new marketplace. Almost by definition, they entered business as entrepreneurs and left it—those who managed to create the enterprises that survived to become fixtures in the American economy—as leaders.

Leadership meant gathering and nurturing businesses that were metropolitan in scale yet scattered across the globe. The challenge for leaders was not just one of organization or management, as vital as these dimensions of the problem were. It was ultimately a question of inspiring, of drawing diverse and dispersed participants into a shared vision, a mutual faith, a common spirit of enterprise.

For some, leadership came naturally. It was integral to their personalities. J. P. Morgan could take over a room simply by walking into it. His physique was splendid, his voice commanding, and his eyes, it was said, were like the headlights of an oncoming train. Even his scabrous nose, scarred by a skin disease, added to an aura that made people fear, respect, and trust him at the same time. P. T. Barnum had an instinct for joyful showmanship, an infectious quality that enabled investors and customers alike to suspend belief and come back for more. John D. Rockefeller, whatever the photographs reveal about his unappealing and austere demeanor, commanded through sheer force of will and intellect. Alfred Sloan, the button-down organization man, just made sense.

But even those entrepreneurs who proved to be natural leaders had to grow into their roles, because leadership in big business had to be leadership on new terms. Organizations like Carnegie Steel, Standard Oil, Ford Motor Company, and General Motors were not just new kinds of businesses but new kinds of communities—new forms of social as well as economic organization. Leading thus meant adapting old truths to new circumstances. How exactly did a chief executive officer set the tone of business, convey the company's mission, inspire hard work and creativity, and measure and reward performance?

And how, beyond the corporation, did the chief executive exercise social leadership? In that respect, the great industrialists were less noteworthy, though they did, in effect, "invent" modern, systematic philanthropy.

The Force of Character

" Business is only a form of teaching. You teach people to desire your product; that is selling. You teach workmen how to make the right product; that is manufacturing. You teach others to cooperate with you; that is organization. "

JOHN HENRY PATTERSON OF NATIONAL CASH REGISTER

In practice, Patterson was authoritarian and hot-tempered. In fact, he drove one of his most important assets—Tom Watson Sr.—out of his company. Watson went on to build IBM. Still, Patterson had captured a fundamental aspect of business leadership.

Mail-order king A. Montgomery Ward put the same point a little differently. Listen to him wax lyrical on what he saw as the key development in his era's most dynamic enterprise:

Thus we find Carnegie founding the steel trust. He throws Carnegie personality into the organization. Carnegie power goes in also. Carnegie guarantee likewise—and we find the steel trust's girders and beams labeled not "United States Steel Corporation," but "Carnegie."

Now, that personality of his influences every employee, stimulates every manager, creates duplication of each good idea upon the broadest plane until each part of the great combination is enjoying the best that each other part has, and finally finds imperishable expression in that lettering on the steel framework of the enormous buildings and bridges and elevated structures which are a greater monument to Carnegie than his libraries.

A. MONTGOMERY WARD

What both Ward and Patterson were describing was the critical challenge of disseminating a vision of the enterprise throughout the organization. Carnegie's steel made a nice metaphor, but ironically, "Carnegie Steel" was destined to be rolled into "U.S. Steel" in 1901, when J. P. Morgan bought out the steelmaker and assembled a far broader, more diffuse organization.

Institutional Identification

General Motors, which was just as broad and just as diffuse as U.S. Steel, could not rely on the magnetism of its founder, ultimately, to build organizational cohesion. In its place, managers like Alfred Sloan cultivated a very different brand of leadership. Sloan scrupulously resisted getting dragged down into the minutia of running the company.

> Of all business activities, 99% are routine. . . . The entire 100% can be handled by managing the 1% of exceptions.
>
> ALFRED SLOAN

But then, even with respect to the 1 percent:

> Every executive has to recognize sooner or later that he himself cannot do everything that needs to be done. Until he recognizes this, he is only an individual, with an individual's power, but after he recognizes it, he becomes, for the first time, an executive, with control of multiple powers.
>
> ALFRED SLOAN

The dictum shaped leadership all along the managerial chain of command at GM. From the boardroom at the very top, one of the company's most important directors proclaimed:

> The right type of [leader] is democratic. He must not consider himself a superior sort of personage. He must actually feel democratic; it is not enough that he try to pose as democratic—he must *be* democratic, otherwise the veneer, the sheen, would wear off, for you can't fool a body of intelligent American workingmen for very long. He must ring true.
>
> T. COLEMAN DU PONT

Sloan could not have agreed more. Yet even that apostle of decentralized decisionmaking and consensus-building spoke to the importance of having one final executive authority.

> Decentralization or not, an industrial corporation is not the mildest form of organization in society. I never minimized the administrative power of the chief executive officer in principle when I occupied that position. I simply exercised that power with discretion; I got better results by selling my ideas than by telling people what to do. Yet the power to act must be located in the chief executive officer.
>
> ALFRED SLOAN

Attracting and Keeping Top Talent

For chief executives to enjoy that power to act, and lead, they also needed to have people willing to follow. Ideally, followers had to be more than "yes-men." The best companies, after all, wanted to attract and retain the best talent.

When people think of business as a mere matter of merchandise, of buying and making and selling goods, they overlook what is perhaps the most important, and certainly the most interesting, factor in the game. It takes men to produce merchandise. It takes men to sell it. To get the right kind of men is, therefore, the chief concern of every executive.

HARVEY FIRESTONE

Take away the gender bias and Firestone's vision of the enterprise was strikingly holistic. Rhetorically, at least, the industrialist was recognizing the significance of what today goes by the name of human capital. Getting it was as critical then as it is now.

Andrew Carnegie put his finger right on it:

There is always a boom in brains, cultivate that crop, for if you grow any amount of that commodity, here is your best market and you cannot overstock it, and the more brains you have to sell, the higher price you can extract.

ANDREW CARNEGIE,
"THE ROAD TO BUSINESS SUCCESS," 1885

Cultivating brains meant nurturing them, not ordering them around dictatorially.

Genius is sensitive in all its forms, and it is unusual, not ordinary, ability that tells even in practical affairs. You must capture and keep the heart of the original and supremely able man before his brain can do his best.

ANDREW CARNEGIE

Carnegie sounded the warning to executives in charge, and he offered an inverted form of the same advice to people below.

You will never be a partner unless you know the business of your department far better than the owners possibly can. When called to account for your independent action, show him the result of your genius, and tell him that you knew that it would be so; show him how mistaken the orders were. Boss your boss just as soon as you can; try it on early. There is nothing he will like so well if he is the right kind of boss; if he is not, he is not the man for you to remain with—leave him whenever you can, even at present sacrifice, and find one capable of discerning genius. Our young partners in the Carnegie firm have won their spurs by showing that we did not know half as well what was wanted as they did. Some of them have acted upon occasion with me as if they owned the firm and I was but some airy New Yorker presuming to advise upon what I knew very little about. Well, they are not interfered with much now. They were the true bosses—the very men we were looking for.

ANDREW CARNEGIE

To make it safe for "genius" to flourish in an organization a leader had to be secure enough not only to delegate authority and credit but also to accept responsibility for problems. Harvey Firestone put it best when he declared:

I hold that, if anything in the business is wrong, the fault is squarely with management. If the tires were not made right, if the workmen are unhappy, if the sales are not what they ought to be, the fault is not with the man who is actually doing the job, but with the men above him and the men above them, so that, finally, the fault is mine. That is my conception of business.

HARVEY FIRESTONE

Creating a Sense of "Ownership"

The early industrialists became notorious for their antagonistic and exploitative attitudes toward their workers. If anything, they seemed bent on proving Marx's theory that a class struggle was inevitable between the owners and managers of production on one side and workers on the other.

The treatment of ordinary labor by managers was abysmal by modern standards. And in unguarded moments the rhetoric matched the treatment.

> Every successful enterprise requires three men—a dreamer, a businessman, and a son-of-a-bitch.
>
> PETER McARTHUR, 1901

(Presumably the last of these was the manager.)

Jay Gould held the workers on his railroads in blatant contempt. He recognized, as few industrialists would openly, that ethnic rivalries ran deep on the shop floor, as each succeeding wave of immigrants worked for lower wages, and that the pressure to find work gave employers powerful possibilities for exploitation.

> I can hire one half the working class to kill the other half.
>
> JAY GOULD, 1886

Even entrepreneurs like Andrew Carnegie regarded their blue-collar employees warily at best, if not as beasts to be driven hard. Carnegie assumed that the gulf dividing the ordinary worker and the leadership of a corporation was an unfortunate but necessary facet of industrialization.

> We assemble thousands of operatives in the factory, and in the mine, of whom the employer can know little or nothing, and to whom he is little better than a myth.
>
> ANDREW CARNEGIE

Depending on one's point of view, the steel magnate sounds either cynical or naive and wistful in declaring:

> If the managing owners and officials of great corporations could only be known to their men and, equally important, their men known to their employers, and the hearts of each exposed to the other, as well as their difficulties, we should have in that troublesome field such harmony as delights us in the domestic.
>
> ANDREW CARNEGIE

Still, when push came to shove at his own Homestead steel mills in 1892, Carnegie took a convenient trip overseas while Henry Clay Frick, his ruthless lieutenant, leveled guns on the striking steelworkers to bring them to heel. Blood flowed at Homestead, and Carnegie's reputation for humane thinking never recovered in his own lifetime.

Other employers, though, began to cast about for more creative solutions and more sustainable kinds of business communities. It made for better public relations. But far more important (as far as the Robber Barons were concerned), it gradually came to seem like sound business too.

Early Experiments in Employee Ownership:
P&G and Kodak

William Cooper Procter confronted the daunting challenge of more deeply investing the company's vast and varied workforce in the enterprise. Procter started working at Procter & Gamble under his father in 1886, when the business was burgeoning in size and breaking down periodically under debilitating outbursts of labor unrest. Between 1886 and 1887 the company struggled to cope with no less than fourteen strikes and an employee turnover rate of 50 percent. Procter recognized the need to distribute something like a sense of ownership across his huge organization. Or as he himself put it, he wanted his employees to think of themselves as "working capitalists."

P&G launched a profit-sharing program, the first of its kind in big business. "Dividend Day" became a key annual event at P&G. And for good measure, Procter set up comprehensive insurance benefits, which were again extraordinary for the time. As Procter saw things:

> The chief problem of "big business" today is to shape its policies so that each worker, whether in office or factory, will feel he is a vital part of his company, with a personal responsibility for its success, and a chance to share in that success.
>
> WILLIAM COOPER PROCTER

In pursuit of this atmosphere of mutual belonging, P&G forged ahead again in 1919 when it implemented a stock ownership program for employees. For as Procter came to feel, "It is more than money that the men want, it is a sense of ownership."

Thus, Procter & Gamble, over the late 1880s and early 1900s, recognized the power of the "sweat equity" principle driving high-tech entrepreneurship today. P&G would eventually be able to point to success stories entirely akin to Microsoft's millionaire secretaries.

At Kodak, George Eastman also worked hard at vesting his people. When the company went public in 1899, the founder made a pile of money. But he felt strongly that the windfall should be shared with everybody who had participated in the venture. And so he organized what he called the "divvy." Every Kodak employee got an extra paycheck, with the following note:

> I have the pleasure to inform you that Mr. Eastman has set aside to commemorate the recent combination of the Kodak business a sum for distribution among the employees of various Kodak companies, to be apportioned according to their time of service, present rate of pay, and the kind of employment. . . . This is a personal matter with Mr. Eastman and he requests that you will not consider it as a gift, but as extra pay for extra good work.
>
> COMPANY LETTER TO KODAK EMPLOYEES, 1899

Kodak had just experienced a nineteenth-century version of an IPO, and Eastman wanted to make sure his employees felt vested in the event and the venture.

Sorting out Corporate Constituencies

> The public be damned.
>
> WILLIAM H. VANDERBILT

They employed workforces numbering in the tens if not the hundreds of thousands. They oversaw the deployment of millions of dollars' worth of investment. They created and strove to satisfy

Making a Community of NCR

It has become fashionable to house modern high-tech companies not in "plants" or "office complexes" but on "campuses." The instinct working here—to create a corporate landscape that suggests a nurturing environment of learning as much as play—has deep historical antecedents. Consider the effort of a company like National Cash Register. Founder and patriarch John H. Patterson was one of the more progressive turn-of-the-century employers. He built clean, well-ventilated, well-lit factories, set in parklike landscapes. He equipped them with lunchrooms, bathrooms with tubs and showers, even a library and classrooms for after-hours classes. He set up lecture series and urged his workers to form social clubs. For Patterson firmly believed:

> It pays to give your employees the full market price for their labor, and then to spend an additional sum for their welfare.

The notion was not only benevolent, it was bottom-line savvy. In Patterson's words: "It is an investment. It pays."

vast markets of consumers. They assumed positions within the social elite. They stirred up bitter social protests. Gradually awareness of the wider implications of industrial enterprise took hold.

The lion of Wall Street was widely reported to have barked, when pressed for comment in the midst of a financial crisis,

" I owe the public nothing. "

J. P. MORGAN

Morgan's response was actually more neutral. But the legend of this retort spread anyway. The fact that it was believed betrayed deep public uneasiness with the power that people like Morgan were accumulating.

If Morgan himself ever felt uneasy about holding vast power or responsibility, he never let on. Other business leaders, however, publicly acknowledged and strove to sort out their various responsibilities.

Golden rule principles are just as necessary for operating a business profitably as are trucks, typewriters, and twine.

James C. Penney, 1902

In a fledgling young financial market for industrial stocks, for example, it took some time to delineate investors' rights from managerial prerogatives. Testifying before Congress in 1899, H. O. Havemeyer, leader of the powerful sugar trust, insisted that financial markets should be unregulated and investors left to fend for themselves. *Caveat emptor.*

> Q: You think . . . that when a corporation is chartered by the state, offers stock to the public, and is one in which the public is interested, that the public has no right to know what its earning power is, . . . that the people may not buy stock blindly?
>
> HAVEMEYER: Yes; that is my theory. Let the buyer beware; that covers the whole business. You cannot wet-nurse people from the time they are born until the day they die. They have to wade in and get stuck and that is the way men are educated and cultivated.

One question quickly became vitally important: on whose behalf were the leaders of large corporations primarily acting? The industrialists struggled with this problem, just as corporate mangers do today. In very large corporations, second-generation executives were not normally major investors in their businesses. They were simply the "agents" of owners, whose holdings were increasingly dispersed. Power thus shifted from owners to managers.

Executives had special responsibilities to shareholders, of course, but they also had to respond to other constituencies as well—their employees, their customers, and the communities in which they operated. Sometimes it was hard to keep focused on what shareholders wanted the most: profit maximization. Writing in 1914, a young journalist noted that:

" [America's big businesses were normally] managed by . . . managers [who] are on salary, divorced from ownership. . . . The motive of profit is not their motive. "

WALTER LIPPMANN

Of course, many owner-managers were also not driven by profits. Henry Ford, who always controlled his company's stock, had remarkably little concern for profits per se. His notion of enterprise was rooted in a larger social vision.

" Business as a money-making game is not worth much thought. It is no place for a man who wants really to accomplish something. Also it is not the best way to make money. The foundation of real business is service. "

HENRY FORD

Stockholders, Ford liked to say, were mere "parasites."

"Incidentally Make Money"

Henry Ford's theory of business so alienated his minority shareholders that they sued him for neglecting their interests in 1917. The automaker's cross-examination went as follows:

Q.: You say you do not think it is right to make so much profits? What is this business being continued for, and why is it being enlarged?

A.: To do as much [good] as possible for everybody concerned.

Q.: What do you mean by "doing as much good as possible"?

A.: To make money and use it, give employment, and send out the car where the people can use it.

Q.: Is that all? Haven't you said that you had money enough yourself, and you were going to run the Ford Motor Company thereafter to em-

(continues)

(continued)

ploy just as many people as you could, to give them the benefits of the high wages that you [p]aid, and to give the public the benefit of a low priced car?

A.: I suppose I have, and incidentally make money.

Q.: Incidentally make money?

A.: Yes sir.

Q.: But your controlling feature, so far as your policy, since you have got all the money you want, is to employ a great army of men at high wages, to reduce the selling price of the car, so that a lot of people can buy it at a cheap price, and give everybody a car that wants one?

A.: If you give all that, the money will fall into your hands; you can't get out of it.

The true industrial idea is not to make money. The industrial idea is to express a serviceable idea, to duplicate a useful idea, by as many thousands as there are people who need it.

Henry Ford, *My Life and Work,* 1922

Sloan, the du Ponts, and many other business leaders disagreed. They focused on maximizing shareholder value and keyed compensation to how well managers generated returns on invested capital. Throughout his career at the head of what became the largest business in the world, Alfred Sloan asked his staff continuously:

" How has the corporation served its owners? I believe this can best be seen by looking at the financial records of the business. "

ALFRED SLOAN, *MY YEARS WITH GENERAL MOTORS*, 1964

But then, Sloan too described the mission of an institution like General Motors as leadership in broad, societal terms.

We like to believe that we have made a contribution as an industrial leader. Employees, shareholders, dealers, consumers, suppliers—and the government to a large degree—have shared in the success of General Motors.

ALFRED SLOAN,
MY YEARS WITH GENERAL MOTORS, 1964

Howard Heinz, the head of the eponymous H. J. Heinz Company, attempted to make his managers shareholders—to keep the interests of his operators closely aligned with those of the enterprise's owners. Articulating what he called the "Spirit of the House" that gave employees a sense of corporate family, Heinz sought to reinforce spirit with tangible ownership benefits.

" The new [employees] ought to understand something about the Spirit of the House. . . . You know ordinarily the idea in the East is that a corporation is a stone-hearted thing that knows nothing but dollars and cents. If I thought this was the kind of organization the H. J. Heinz Company was I would quit my job today . . . neither do I expect you to work for such an organization. . . . Classed a corporation . . . it is nothing more or less than a partnership in which there are some members of the family, in addition to about 30 men grown up in this business. We have presented them with stock. There isn't a man who cannot get stock if he has the ability and character. . . . I mean to " say that it is a business that belongs to the employees. . . . It is just as much your business as it is my Heinz.

HOWARD HEINZ

The Business Leader as Social Force

A funny thing happened on the way to fortune. "Robbers"—some of them anyway—became "Barons." Men like Henry Ford were not necessarily bent on getting rich—but they did. As they built up business empires, hard-driving industrialists acquired vast personal wealth. They became so rich, in fact, that their holdings dwarfed those of the country's traditional elite.

Some considered it a burden thrust upon them by good fortune. Leland Stanford, for example, used a substantial chunk of the fortune he made in railroads to endow the university that bore his name, proclaiming:

> " The advantages of wealth are greatly exaggerated. "
>
> LELAND STANFORD

Most people would prefer to bear the burden. Still, it posed problems of its own. What should be done with money that so vastly exceeded one's needs? Some found ways to spend it on themselves, to be sure. But others searched for more meaningful ways to spend their fortunes. The man who built Coca-Cola wrote to his brother, a Methodist bishop:

> " I never keep money. Money is not meant to be hoarded. Myself and all I have I try to keep righteously active. "
>
> ASA CANDLER

Andrew Carnegie was not merely content to say that you can't take it with you. It was evil even to try.

> " Surplus wealth is a sacred trust which its possessor is bound to administer in his lifetime for the good of the community. "
>
> ANDREW CARNEGIE

Or, as the steelmaker put it more bluntly:

> " The man who dies . . . rich, dies disgraced. "
>
> ANDREW CARNEGIE

The Evils of Inherited Wealth

Andrew Carnegie was not alone in his concern that wealth transferred from one generation to the next within families was wealth squandered. If nothing else, it defeated the principle of merit. (Carnegie reportedly said, "From shirtsleeves to shirtsleeves in three generations.") And from the vantage point of the beneficiary, inherited wealth was not always a blessing. Listen to the third generation of the once-great Vanderbilt business dynasty.

> Inherited wealth is a big handicap to happiness. It is as certain death to ambition as cocaine is to immorality.
>
> WILLIAM K. VANDERBILT

It was biblical, if nothing else. Indeed, more devout businesspeople (Carnegie was actually more of a secular humanist) saw themselves as having been charged with a special, moral obligation to act as stewards of wealth in this life. Most famously (or infamously, depending on one's point of view), John D. Rockefeller drew on his pious Baptist faith to justify the fortune his business had brought him.

I believe the power to make money is a gift of God
. . . to be developed and used to the best of our ability
for the good of mankind. Having been endowed with
the gift I possess, I believe it is my duty to make money
and still more money, and to use this money I make
for the good of my fellow men according to the dic-
tates of my conscience.

JOHN D. ROCKEFELLER

Rockefeller, you know, is reputed the richest man in the
world, and he certainly is the most powerfully suggestive
personality I have ever seen. A man 10 stories deep, and to
me quite unfathomable. Physionomie de Pierrot (not a
spear of hair on head or face), flexible, cunning, quakerish,
superficially suggestive of naught but goodness and consci-
entiousness, yet accused of being the greatest villain in business whom our country as produced.

William James, 1904

Whatever the faith behind it, industrial philanthropy required
just as much inventiveness and resourcefulness as industrial business—at least in the hands of the imaginatively conscientious.
Rockefeller, Carnegie, Ford, and company built new kinds of businesses, and then they built new kinds of charitable institutions.
They invented modern, systematically organized philanthropies,
leaving behind great foundations that bear their names.

Rockefeller, for example, followed the logic of one of his pet
projects, medical philanthropy:

The best philanthropy is constantly in search of the fi-
nalities—a search for cause, an attempt to cure evils at
their source.

JOHN D. ROCKEFELLER

Historical Echo: "The Gospel of Wealth"

Only recently have the rising millionaires and billionaires of the New Economy begun to wrestle with the question of how to deploy their fortunes. Bill Gates's commitment to establishing the foundation in his name bears more than a passing resemblance to Rockefeller's actions a century earlier. Each entrepreneur became one of the richest people of his day, and both did so in the course of assembling businesses that monopolized their industries. Both were as infamous, in the end, as they were rich. Rockefeller's charity only partially redeemed his name; Gates's fate, of course, remains to be determined.

But the classic voice on the subject of converting from industrial (or postindustrial) tycoon into philanthropist was not Rockefeller's but Andrew Carnegie's. In 1868 the young railroad superintendent sat down and scratched out an extraordinary personal memorandum to himself:

> Thirty three and an income of 50,000$ per annum. By this time in two years I can arrange all my business as to secure at least 50,000 per annum. Beyond this never earn—make no effort to increase fortune, but spend the surplus each year for benovelent [*sic*] purposes. Cast aside business forever except for others. . . . Man must have an idol—The amassing of wealth is one of the worst species of idolitary [*sic*]. No idol more debasing than the worship of money. Whatever I engage in I must push inordinately therefore I should be careful to choose that life which will be the most elevating in its character.
>
> ANDREW CARNEGIE

Carnegie promptly filed the memo and went back to work. In fact, he would spend several more decades in busi-

(continues)

(continued)

ness, "push[ing] inordinately" and multiplying both his fortune and his income several times over in the steel industry. When he sold out to J. P. Morgan's U.S. Steel, Morgan congratulated him on being the richest man in the world. Carnegie had not entirely forgotten his youthful resolve, however. In the years following his retirement from business he did indeed methodically give away all but a small portion of his personal wealth (leaving only a modest amount to his only daughter) in organizations he established to promote education, world peace, and literacy.

The problem of our age is the proper administration of wealth, that the ties of brotherhood may still bind together the rich and poor in harmonious relationship.

. . . This, then, is held to be the duty of the man of wealth: To set an example of modest, unostentatious living, shunning display or extravagance; to provide moderately for the legitimate wants of those dependent upon him; and, after doing so, to consider all surplus revenues which come to him simply as trust funds, which he is called upon to administer, and strictly bound as a matter of duty to administer in the manner which, in his judgment, is best calculated to produce the most beneficial results for the community—the man of wealth thus becoming the mere trustee and agent for his poorer brethren, bringing to their service his superior wisdom, experience, and ability to administer, doing for them better than they would or could do for themselves.

ANDREW CARNEGIE,
"GOSPEL OF WEALTH," 1889

However much social responsibility the great industrialists were willing to accept, by the 1920s it was clear they had come to dominate American life as earlier generations of businesspeople never had. No less an authority than the president of the United States announced the fact.

"   The chief business of the American people is Business.   "
                                                      CALVIN COOLIDGE

To which the great advertising pioneer Bruce Barton added an exceptionally thoughtful postscript. The successful operation of an enterprise, he reminded his readers, had made the successful entrepreneurs of the age leaders, whether they wanted to acknowledge the role or not.

"   The American business man is . . . the most influential
    person in the nation . . . perhaps in the world. . . . This
    means that he is on trial. . . . Business heretofore has
    been permitted to concern itself exclusively with the
    practical details of business. . . . The question now is
    will and can the business . . . leader concern himself
    with more . . . and, in addition, make noteworthy con-
    tributions to civilization.   "
                                                      BRUCE BARTON

CHRONOLOGY:
BIG BUSINESS, HIGH TECHNOLOGY, AND WORLD EVENTS,
1870–1929

DATE	BUSINESS	TECHNOLOGY	WORLD EVENTS
1870			Franco-Prussian War breaks out.
1872	Aaron Montgomery Ward establishes Montgomery Ward & Company, issuing a one-page leaflet as its first mail-order catalog.		
	Andrew Carnegie begins building the Edgar Thomson Steel Mills.		
	John D. Rockefeller consolidates a dominant position in Cleveland's (and therefore the world's) oil-refining industry.		
1876		Alexander Graham Bell obtains the first U.S. patent for the telephone.	Queen Victoria takes the title Empress of India.

DATE	BUSINESS	TECHNOLOGY	WORLD EVENTS
1876 (cont.)		Thomas Edison invents a mimeograph device, the first practical duplicating machine.	
1877		Edison shouts "Mary had a little lamb" into a device, thereby producing the first recorded and reproduced sound.	Major strike paralyzes national railroad network. State and national guards are mobilized to put down the strike.
1878	Edison forms the Edison Electric Light Company.	A commercial telephone exchange goes into operation in New Haven, Connecticut—the first regularly operating switchboard system in the nation.	The Treaty of Berlin partitions the former Ottoman Empire, temporarily maintaining peace in Europe.
1879	Procter & Gamble develops Ivory Soap.	James T. Riley, a saloon-keeper, invents the first cash register.	
		Edison invents the incandescent lamp.	

1881	Chicago meatpacker Gustavus Swift hires Andrew Chase to design a refrigerated railroad car to carry dressed beef to eastern cities.	Edison constructs the world's first central electric power plant on Pearl Street in New York City.	
	James Buchanan Duke converts plant from chewing tobacco to cigarette production.		
1882	John D. Rockefeller establishes the Standard Oil Trust, an umbrella organization coordinating operations on the forty different oil companies he controls.		
1884			For the first time, the United States outstrips England in steel production.
1885		German manufacturer Karl Benz builds the prototype for the first gasoline-powered automobile.	

DATE	BUSINESS	TECHNOLOGY	WORLD EVENTS
1886		Charles Martin Hall invents a process for producing pure aluminum inexpensively.	Samuel Gompers and other labor leaders found the American Federation of Labor.
1888	Sears, Roebuck and Company sends out its first mail-order catalog.		
	Asa Candler gains legal control of Coca-Cola, a pharmaceutical concoction invented by Atlanta chemist John Pemberton.		
	George Eastman introduces the Kodak, the first camera simple enough for even amateurs to use.		
1889	Carnegie publishes *Gospel of Wealth*.		
1890	James Buchanan Duke establishes the American Tobacco Corporation.		

1892	A strike at Carnegie's Homestead mills ends in violence when management brings in a force of armed Pinkerton security agents to disperse worker pickets.			
	The Edison Electric Company and a rival merge to form the General Electric Company.			
1896	Henry Ford builds his first car, the "quadricycle."			
1901	Carnegie sells his steel operations to J. P. Morgan's steel syndicate. Morgan goes on to organize U.S. Steel, the world's first billion-dollar corporation. Carnegie retires to devote himself to philanthropy.			
1902		Arthur D. Little patents rayon.		

DATE	BUSINESS	TECHNOLOGY	WORLD EVENTS
1903	Ford organizes the Ford Motor Company.	The Wright brothers successfully launch a power-driven flying machine at Kitty Hawk, North Carolina.	
	William Durant forms General Motors, merging Oldsmobile and Buick.		
1904–1905			Russo-Japanese War establishes Japan as a world power.
1906	Carnegie founds his Foundation for the Advancement of Teaching—"to do all things necessary to encourage, uphold, and dignify the profession of teaching." This is one of several great philanthropic efforts to redistribute his accumulated wealth.	Reginald Fessenden makes the first known radio broadcast of voice and music.	
1907	U.S. government initiates antitrust action against explosives maker E. I. du Pont de Nemours and Company, precipitating company to expand into other chemical markets.		

119

1907 (cont.)	Morgan organizes a coalition of New York financiers to provide liquidity to the nation's leading banks during the 1907 banking panic. The effect of his intervention leads Congress to consider establishing what would become the Federal Reserve		
1908	Carnegie founds his Foundation for the Advancement of Teaching—"to do all things necessary to encourage, uphold, and dignify the profession of teaching." This is one of several great philanthropic efforts to redistribute his accumulated wealth.		
	The Ford Motor Company introduces the Model T.		
	Morgan considers, and rejects, an offer from Durant to underwrite a share of General Motors.		

DATE	BUSINESS	TECHNOLOGY	WORLD EVENTS
1908 (cont.)	Durant incorporates General Motors Company of New Jersey.		
1909	Cadillac and Oakland (renamed Pontiac) join General Motors.	First wireless message travels from New York City to Chicago. Leo H. Baekeland announces development of Bakelite, a thermosetting resin that, because of its extremely high electrical resistance, will be used to make insulators and other components for the electrical and later the radio industry.	
1910			Japan annexes Korea.

1911	Henry Leland, head of Cadillac (a division of General Motors), demonstrates the first electric automotive self-starter.	
	The Supreme Court dissolves the American Tobacco Company as an illegal monopoly and orders the breakup of Standard Oil into thirty-four separate companies.	
	Carnegie establishes the Carnegie Corporation.	
1912		Establishment of the Republic of China under Sun Yat-sen marks the end of the Manchu Dynasty.
	Swiss factories begin producing cellophane and cellulose film; the DuPont Corporation buys the American production rights in 1923.	The "unsinkable" *Titanic* sinks within hours of striking an iceberg.

DATE	BUSINESS	TECHNOLOGY	WORLD EVENTS
1913	Ford installs a moving assembly line in his factory.		
	The Rockefeller Foundation, established "to promote the well-being of mankind throughout the world," is chartered in New York.		
1914		For the first time, an American, William Richards, wins a Nobel Prize in Chemistry, for his work in determining the exact atomic weights of a number of elements.	The assassination of Archduke Ferdinand sparks World War I.
1915		Bell, speaking from New York City, makes the first transcontinental telephone call, to Dr. Thomas A. Watson in San Francisco.	

1915 (cont.)		Edison announces the invention of the "telescribe" to record telephone conversations.
1916	Henry Ford begins constructing the River Rouge plant.	
1917			US enters World War I.
			Lenin seizes power in Russia.
			Balfour Declaration supports the idea of Jewish state in Palestine.
1918		First airmail service begins with regular flights between New York City and Washington, D.C.	
1919	In the face of investor opposition to his ambitious plans for expansion, Ford buys up all outstanding shares of the Ford Motor Company, taking it private.		At the Paris Peace Conference, the United States, Great Britain, France, and Italy draft the Versailles Treaty, ending World War I.

DATE	BUSINESS	TECHNOLOGY	WORLD EVENTS
1919 (cont.)	General Electric, AT&T, Westinghouse, and other major corporations pool radio patents to form the Radio Corporation of America (RCA).		
1920	In the midst of a sharp recession, the du Ponts remove Durant as head of General Motors and reorganize the company under Alfred Sloan.		
	Westinghouse begins operating the first commercial radio broadcasting station, KDKA, in Pittsburgh.	Rail mileage in the United States reaches its all-time peak of 253,000.	
1922		The New York City telephone system installs the first mechanical switchboard.	
1923		Lee De Forest, "the father of radio," demonstrates a sound motion picture process called Phonofilm.	

1923 (cont.)		Colonel Jacob Stick receives a patent for the first electric shaver.	
1924	For the first time, General Motors outpaces Ford Motor Company in earnings; by 1929 GM will also be selling more cars than Ford.	RCA demonstrates wireless transmission of photographs from London to New York City.	
1927	Shortly after making its fifteen-millionth Model T, Ford Motor Company takes the extraordinary step of shutting down its factories for six months to retool for a new Model A.	Television successfully demonstrated for the first time.	
1928		Eastman Kodak exhibits the first color motion pictures in the United States at Rochester, New York.	
1929	Stock market crash anticipates the Great Depression.		Lieutenant Commander Richard E. Bird completes the first flight over the South Pole.

FURTHER READING

Andrew Carnegie

Carnegie composed numerous essays, several of them highly influential in his day. Late in life the steel magnate wrote up an extensive set of notes as a preliminary draft of a memoir; though he eventually dropped the project, the notes were arranged and published posthumously as *Autobiography of Andrew Carnegie* (Boston: Houghton Mifflin Company, 1920). The best one-volume biography of Carnegie is Joseph Frazier Wall, *Andrew Carnegie* (Pittsburgh: University of Pittsburgh Press, 1970). Harold Livesay's more incisive *Andrew Carnegie and the Rise of Big Business* (Boston: Little, Brown and Company, 1975) is also worth reading.

Thomas Edison

Paul Israel's *Edison: A Life of Invention* (New York: John Wiley, 1998) offers a good biographical portrait. For a firsthand account of the inventor by one of his lab assistants, see Francis Jehl, *Menlo Park Reminiscences* (Dearborn, Mich.: Edison Institute, 1936). Four volumes of a comprehensive, multivolume collection of Edison's papers have been published: *The Papers of Thomas A. Edison,* edited by Reese V. Jenkins et al. (Baltimore: Johns Hopkins University Press, 1989).

Henry Ford

Ford wrote, or at least put his name to, a constant stream of essays and little books, many of them probably composed in collaboration with ghostwriters. The best place to start is the vivid memoir he wrote with Samuel Crowther, *My Life and Work* (Garden City, N.Y.: Garden City Publishing Company, 1922). See also the account written by one of Ford's most important managers, Charles E. Sorensen, with Samuel T. Williamson, *My Forty Years with Ford* (New York: W. W. Norton, 1956).

J. P. Morgan

J. Pierpont Morgan truly lived by the credo: "Think a lot. Say little. Write nothing." He left nothing like a memoir. Several insightful secondary studies are available, however, including Ron Chernow's sweeping account of the family and its banks, *The House of Morgan: An American Banking Dynasty and the Rise of Modern Finance* (New York: Atlantic Monthly Press, 1990); and Jean Strouse, *Morgan: American Financier* (New York: Random House, 1999), which draws a fine psychological portrait.

John D. Rockefeller

Rockefeller's *Random Reminiscences of Men and Events* (New York: Doubleday, Page & Company, 1909) is a classic text in business history and a fascinating self-portrait. The account the oil tycoon offers of himself and his business is generally engaging, sometimes revealing, but also disingenuous about critical aspects of Standard Oil's ascent to dominance. For a roughly contemporary account from a sharply critical perspective, see Ida M. Tarbell, *The History of the Standard Oil Company* (New York: McClure, Phillips, 1905), along with a pair of articles the muckraker published in *McClure's Magazine* in July and August 1905, "John D. Rockefeller: A Character Study." The best recent biography is Ron Chernow, *Titan: The Life of John D. Rockefeller Sr.* (New York: Random House, 1998).

Alfred Sloan

Measured, sober, yet leavened with his distinctive dry wit, Sloan's *My Years with General Motors* (Garden City, N.Y.: Doubleday, 1964) is another classic business memoir. It remains a powerfully insightful, highly relevant treatise on management.

Other Robber Barons

Phineas T. Barnum, perhaps the most flamboyant entrepreneur of the nineteenth century, wrote an autobiography that has recently been reissued: *The Life of P. T. Barnum, Written by Himself,* edited by Terence Whelan (Champaign: University of Illinois Press, 2000). See also Neil Harris's biography *Humbug: The Art of P. T. Barnum* (Boston: Little, Brown and Company, 1973).

A minor classic, Harvey Firestone's *Men and Rubber* (with Samuel Crowther) (Garden City, N.Y.: Doubleday, Page & Co., 1926) was written by an entrepreneur as iconoclastic as his most important customer, Henry Ford.

Besides Tarbell's work on Rockefeller, other social critics of the Robber Barons are included in Donald P. DeNevi and Helen M. Friend's useful anthology, *Muckrakers and Robber Barons: The Classic Era, 1902–1912* (Danville, Calif.: Replica Books, 1973).

General Business History

For a group portrait of the entrepreneurs of the industrial age, the starting point is Matthew Josephson's *The Robber Barons: The Great American Capitalists, 1861–1901* (New York: Harcourt, Brace and Company, 1934). Josephson's take on his subjects is decidedly unsympathetic; Burton W. Fulsone provides a counter-polemic in *The Myth of the Robber Barons* (Herndon, Va.: Young

America's Foundation, 1991). Jonathan R. T. Hughes, in *The Vital Few: American Economic Progress and Its Protagonists* (Boston: Houghton Mifflin Company, 1965), offers a more balanced and highly readable account that encompasses the major figures. And finally, for a general business history of the period, the most important work is by Alfred D. Chandler, especially *The Visible Hand: The Managerial Revolution in American Business* (Cambridge, Mass.: Harvard University Press, 1977).

INDEX

Accounting, 31(box), 41, 42, 86
    cost accounting, 73
Advertising, 56(box), 57(box), 58,
    61–62, 63
Alcoa, 21–22, 77
Aluminum, 21–22, 33, 77(box), 116
Amazon.com, 17(box), 18
American Federation of Labor, 116
American Museum, 32, 59
American Tobacco Company, 117,
    119
American Union Telephone
    Company, 12
America On Line, 56(box)
Animal by-products, 39(box)
Antitrust actions, 118, 119
Apple Computer, 23(box), 25(box)
Armour, J. Ogden, xi, 39(box)
Armour, Philip, 48
Artificial leather, 50–51
Assembly lines, 40, 119. ISee alsoI
    Mass production
AT&T, 12–13, 120
Authority, 80, 82, 93, 95
Autobiography (Carnegie), 6, 7, 8,
    43
Automobiles, 34, 64, 117
    used-car trade-ins, 65
    See also Ford Motor Company;
    General Motors; Model T
    automobiles

Baekeland, Leo H., 118
Bakelite, 118
Banks/bankers, 22, 30–31, 44, 118.
    See also Investment bankers
Barnum, Phineas T., 32–33, 59, 90
    autobiography of, 125
Barrels, 42
Barton, Bruce, 111
Bell, Alexander Graham, 11–12, 115,
    119
Benz, Karl, 116
Bezos, Jeff, 17–18(box), 49
Big Money, The (Dos Passos), 40(box)
Blame, 77
Boycotts, 48, 53
Brands, 24, 36, 61–63
Bridges, James, 45
Brown, Donaldson, 84–85
Bureaucracies. See
    Managers/management,
    managerial bureaucracies
Burlington, Quincy, and Chicago
    Railroad, 73
By-products, 39(box), 41
Byrd, Richard E., 121

Candler, Asa, 62, 106, 117
Capital, 68, 104
    capital intensive businesses, 21, 73
    human capital, 68(box), 69, 94
    raising, 25–32, 44, 89

Carnegie, Andrew, x, 5–8, 35, 91, 115, 117, 118
  books about, 123. *See also*
    Autobiography (Carnegie);
    "Gospel of Wealth"
  and employees, 96–97
  on human capital, 94–95
  as Napoleonic, 43
  quotes, 6, 7, 8, 36, 37–38, 43—44, 49, 68, 70, 94–95, 97, 107, 109, 110
  and rivals, 46
  on wealth, 107, 109, 110
Carnegie Corporation, 119
Carnegie Steel, 44, 46, 90
  and U.S. Steel, 92, 110
Case, Steve, 56–57(box)
Caveat emptor, 102
Central Savings and Trust Company of Akron, 28
Change, ix, x, xi, 1–2, 2–5, 65
  bureaucratic, 68
  Ford on, 2–3
  vs. routine, 74
  technological, 1, 6, 68
Chase, Andrew, 116
Chemistry, 7–8, 21, 35, 119
Chewing gum, 56–57(box), 64, 78
Christy, Will, 28–29
Chronology, 115–121
Cigarettes, 57–58, 116
Cisco, 13
Clark, Jim, 28
Clark, John Maurice, 20(box)
Class struggle, 96
Cleveland, Ohio, 26, 46–47, 115
Coal, 43, 44, 50(box), 51
Coca-Cola, 61–62, 106, 117
Coke, 43, 44, 51
Committees, 76–77, 87, 88
Competition, 35–65, 73
  competitive advantage, 36, 55, 64
Computers, 23(box), 25(box), 55
Conflicts of interest, 72(box)
Conrad, Frank, 16

Consumers/consumer goods, 24, 35, 54, 55, 57, 59, 61, 64, 100
Coolidge, Calvin, 111
Cooperatives, 18
Corporations, ix, 7, 79, 97, 102
  autonomy of divisions in, 86, 88
  corporate ownership, 49, 96–97, 98–99, 102, 105–106
  corporate raiders, 75
  first billion-dollar corporation, 117
  as nurturing environment, 100(box)
  and Spirit of the House, 105
Correspondence, written, 76, 77(box)
Cosmopolitan magazine, 37, 44
Costs, 64
  cost accounting, 73
  of oil barrels, 42
  production, 20, 21, 37, 38
Creativity, 68, 81, 90
  creative destruction, 2

David, Harry P. 16
Debt, 75
Decision making, 80, 83
  decentralized, 93. *See also*
    Managers/management, centralized/decentralized management
  by groups, 87, 88
De Forest, Lee, 121
Demand, 19, 20, 21, 55, 64, 85
Department heads, 80
Department stores, 19
Depressions, 57(box). *See also* Great Depression
Details, 36–38, 42, 73, 84(box)
Dickinson, Arthur Lowes, 22–23
Discount retailers, 53–54
Distribution, 36, 41, 52, 54–55, 85
Dos Passos, John, 40(box)
Downsizing, ix
Drexel Morgan bank, 14
Duke, James Buchanan, x, 57–58, 116, 117

Du Pont family, x, 93, 104. *See also* E.
    I. du Pont de Nemours
    Company
Du Pont, T. Coleman, 93
Durant, William "Billy," 83, 84(box),
    118, 120

Eastern seaboard, 48
Eastman, George, 24–25, 33, 79, 99,
    117
Eastman Kodak, 121
Economies of scale, 36, 44, 52, 53,
    73
Edgar Thomson Steel Mills, 45, 67,
    115
Edison, Thomas, 8–11, 14, 29–31, 33,
    115, 116, 120
    books about, 123
    quotes, 8, 9–10, 31(box), 34
Edison Electric Light Company, 14,
    32, 115, 117
Edison Phonograph Works, 31
Efficiency, 39(box), 67, 74, 75
E. I. du Pont de Nemours Company,
    36, 80, 81, 118, 119
Electricity, 6, 12, 35, 51
    electric lights, 10, 14–15
    electric power industries, 74
Employment, 2, 55, 89
    employee ownership, 98–99,
        105–106
    Henry Ford on, 103–104(box)
    hiring outsiders, 70, 71, 72(box)
    lay-offs, 75
    treatment of employees, 96, 97, 98,
        99
    turnover rate, 98
    See also Strikes; Talent,
        hiring/retaining
Endowments, x, 106, 109, 118. *See
    also* Philanthropy
Erie Railroad, 72–73
Ethnic rivalries, 96
Expansion, 41–43, 48, 55, 84,
    103(box). *See also* Growth
Experimentation, 10, 50, 55, 74

Experts, 76
Exploitation, 96

Fabbri, Egisto, 71
Federal government, 13
Federal Reserve system, 118
Fessenden, Reginald, 118
Fickes, Edwin, 77
Financial control, 49–50
Financial markets, 25, 102. *See also*
    Stocks
Firestone, Harvey, 33–34, 49–50,
    51–52, 60–61, 125
    and bureaucratic routine,
        76–77
    on growth, 89
    quotes, 3(box), 28–29, 32, 33, 38,
        50, 52, 61, 68, 76–77, 89, 94, 95
    on responsibility, 95
Flivver King, The (Sinclair), 50(box)
Floor sweepings, 38–39
Flow, 36, 43–45, 52, 55
Ford, Henry, 2–5, 21, 29, 33, 38–39,
    50–52, 117
    books by and about, 124
    and business bureaucracies, 81–82,
        87
    buying shares of Ford Motor
        Company, 120
    and investors, 50
    on profits, 103, 103–104(box)
    quotes, x, 1, 2, 3, 4, 19, 20, 35, 39,
        40, 50–51, 64, 78(box), 81–82,
        103, 104
    sister of, 3–4
    See also Ford Motor Company
Ford Motor Company, 29, 60,
    84(box), 90, 117, 118
    vs. General Motors, 81, 121
    River Rouge Plant, 50–51, 67,
        120
    See also Ford, Henry; Model T
        automobiles
Fortune magazine, 84(box), 88
Foundation for the Advancement of
    Teaching, 118

Fox Film, 84(box)
Frick, Henry Clay, 70, 97
Frick Coke Company, 43

Gamble, James, 62. *See also* Procter
     and Gamble
Gates, Bill, 109
General Electric, 9, 32, 117, 120
General Motors, 5, 36, 64–65, 79, 82,
     90, 92, 105, 118, 120
   Buick division of, 86, 118
   vs. Ford Motor Company, 81,
     121
   before Sloan, 84(box)
   See also Sloan, Alfred
Gillette, King, 16–17
Golden rule, 101(box)
Goldsmith, Sir James, 75
Gompers, Samuel, 116
Goodrich, Benjamin Franklin, 15
"Gospel of Wealth" (Carnegie), 110,
     111, 117
Gould, Jay, 74, 75, 96
Grange movement, 18
Great Chicago Fire, 18
Great Depression, 82, 121
Growth, xi, 49, 74, 89. *See also*
     Expansion

Hall, Charles Martin, 21, 22, 116
Haskell, Henry, 81
Havemeyer, H. O., 102
Heinz, Howard, 105–106
History, viii
   business history, 125–126
   historical echoes, 17–19(box),
     23–25(box), 53–54, 75,
     109–110
History of the Standard Oil Company
     (Tarbell), 42
H. J. Heinz Company, 105–106
Homestead steel mills, 97, 117
Honesty, 60, 62
Human capital. *See also* Capital
Hunt, Alfred, 22
Hyatt Roller Bearing company, 83

IBM, 91
Icahn, Carl, 75
Immigrants, 2, 96
Improvisation, 2
Incomes, 65, 104(box), 109
Individualism, 84(box)
Industrial Age, xi, 1, 9, 20, 36, 40, 89
Inflation, 20
Information systems, 78–79, 84, 85,
     86
Inheritance, 107(box)
Innovations, 5, 7, 65, 80
Installment selling, 65
Insull, Samuel, 8
Insurance, 98
Intel, 13
Internet, 13, 17(box)
Intuition, 83
Inventories, 85
Inventors, 9, 10, 22
Investment bankers, 14, 71
Investments/investors, 49, 50, 68, 99,
     100(box), 104, 120
   speculative, vii, 22; *See also*
     Venture capital
Iron, 7, 8, 37, 43, 44, 50(box), 51
Ironton Railway, 51
Ivory soap, 63, 116

James, William, 108(box)
Japan, 118, 119
Jehl, Francis, 29–31
Jobs, 2. *See also* Employment
Jobs, Steve, 23(box)
Johnson, Edward, 15

KDKA radio station, 16, 120
Kettering, Charles F. "Boss," 5
Kodak cameras, 24–25, 33, 99, 117

Labor. *See* Employment
Leadership, 89–111
   social, 90, 105, 106–111
Lefferts, Marshall, 29–30
Leland, Henry, 119
Lemlein, Asa, 58
Lewis, Alfred Henry, 40(box), 44, 47

Limestone, 44
Lippmann, Walter, 102
Literary Digest, 45
Little, Arthur D., 117
Loyalty, 70
Luxuries/necessities, 20

McArthur, Peter, 96
McCallum, Daniel C., 73
Macintosh computers, 23(box)
Mail-order catalogs, 18–19, 52, 53–54,
    67, 115, 117
Managers/management, 46, 49, 50,
    67–88, 89, 96, 97, 102, 104
    centralized/decentralized
        management, 86, 87, 88,
        92–93
    and corporate raiders, 75
    democratic method applied to, 88
    general managers, 72–73
    and information, 79
    managerial bureaucracies, 67–68,
        72–79
    and owners, 102
    as shareholders, 105–106
    Sloan on, 83–88
Marketing strategies, 60, 63. *See also*
        Advertising; Premium
        incentives;
        Salesmanship/salesmen
Markets, ix, 1, 16, 18, 41
    competing in new, 55–58, 59, 61,
        89
    creating new, 19–25, 35, 48, 55
    hinterland, 54(box)
    segmentation of, 65
    shifts in, 64–65
    See also Financial markets
Marx, Karl, 96
Mass production, 35, 36, 52. *See also*
        Assembly lines
Media, vii. *See also* Radio broadcasts;
        Television
Mellon, Andrew and Richard, 22
Men and Rubber (Firestone), 3(box),
    28–29, 32, 38, 50, 52, 61, 89, 125

Menlo Park, 9–10
Menlo Park Reminiscences (Jehl),
    29–31
Metallurgy, 6, 35. *See also* Aluminum;
    Steel
Microsoft, 98
Model T automobiles, 5, 20, 33,
    50(box), 64, 65, 118, 121
Monopolies, 42, 109, 119
Montgomery Ward, 18–19, 52, 115
Morgan, J. P., x, 14, 70–71, 90, 92,
    100–101, 110, 117, 118
    books about, 124
    quotes, 7(box), 71, 100
    wife of, 15
Motion pictures, sound/color, 121
Motor World, 84(box)
My Life and Work (Ford), 1, 4,
    78(box), 82, 104
My Philosophy of Industry (Ford), 3
My Years with General Motors (Sloan),
    5, 85, 86, 87, 88, 105, 125

National Cash Register, 91, 100(box)
Netscape, 13
Networks, 1, 18, 62
New Economy, 109
Newspapers, 53
New York Life Insurance Company,
    72(box)
Nobel Prize, 119

Observation, 9–10
Oil, 35, 38. *See also* Rockefeller, John
    D.; Standard Oil company
Orton, William, 12
Overproduction, 85
Ownership. *See* Corporations,
    corporate ownership

Packaged meats industry, 35, 39(box).
    See also Swift, Gustavus
Palmer, Potter, 19–20
P&G. *See* Procter and Gamble
Passing the buck, 77(box), 78(box)
Patents, 28
Patterson, John Henry, 91, 100(box)

Pemberton, John, 61–62, 117
Penney, James C., 101(box)
Perkins, Charles, 73
Perkins, George W., 72(box)
Personality, 91
Philanthropy, 90, 108, 109, 117, 118.
    See also Endowments
Photography, 24–25
Pickens, T. Boone, 75
Premium incentives, 56(box), 58
Prentis, Meyer, 86
Prices, 20, 47, 51, 52, 53, 54(box), 64,
    104(box)
    of aluminum, 21
    of stocks, 75
Price Waterhouse, 22
Procter, Harley, 63
Procter, William Cooper, 98
Procter & Gamble (P&G), 36, 54–55,
    62–63, 64, 98, 116
Profits, 54(box), 64, 70, 102
    Henry Ford on, 103, 103–104(box)
    profit sharing, 98
Progress, 5, 6, 8, 34, 84(box)
Promotions, 70, 71
Public relations, 97
Pulitzer, Joseph, 75

Quality control, 77

Radio broadcasts, 15–16, 118, 120
Radio Corporation of America
    (RCA), 120, 121
Railroads, 1, 7, 46, 51, 106, 115
    rail mileage, 120
    refrigerated cars, 48, 116
    and rise of business bureaucracy,
    72–74
R&D. *See* Research and development
*Random Reminiscences of Men and
    Events* (Rockefeller), 26, 27,
    41–42
Raw materials, 36, 43, 44, 50, 52
Rayon, 117
RCA. *See* Radio Corporation of
    America

Red tape, 74, 81
Research and development (R&D), 5,
    7
Responsibility, 78(box), 80, 95, 98,
    101, 102, 111
Richards, William, 119
Riley, James T., 116
Risk, xi, 1, 7, 27
Rivals, 46–47
Rockefeller, John D., x, 35, 40(box),
    68–69, 90, 115, 116
    books about, 124. *See also* Random
    Reminiscences of Men and Events
    as Napoleonic, 42
    quotes, ix, 26, 27, 38, 41–42,
    45(caption), 46–47, 69, 108
    and rivals, 46–47
    on wealth, 107–108
Rockefeller Foundation, 119
Rogers, Will, 4(box)
Roses, 45
Rothschild, House of, 71
Ruddiman, Margaret Ford, 3–4
Rural storekeepers, 53–54

Salesmanship/salesmen, 55, 59, 60,
    61, 85
Schumpeter, Joseph, 2
Schwab, Charles, 13–14
Sears, Richard W., 52, 53, 74
Sears, Roebuck and Company, 52,
    53–54, 67, 117
Service sector, 22
Shareholders. *See under* Stocks
Showmanship, 59, 90
Silicon Valley, 28
Sinclair, Upton, 50(box)
Slaughtering production lines,
    39(box)
Sloan, Alfred, x, 64–65, 82, 90,
    104–105, 120, 125
    on management, 83–88, 92, 93
    quotes, 5, 65, 83, 85, 86, 87, 88, 92,
    93, 105
Smelting process, 21, 77(box)
Soap, 63, 64, 116

Specialization, 67
Stagnation, 74–78
Standard Oil Company, 26–27, 41–42, 46, 69, 90
  assimilation of competitors by, 47
  breakup of, 119
  See also Rockefeller, John D.
Standard Oil Trust, 116
Stanford, Leland, 106
Steel, 7, 35, 50(box), 110, 116
  Bessemer process, 6
  manufacturing of, 36–37, 43, 44
  See also Carnegie, Andrew; Edgar Thomson Steel Mills
Stick, Jacob, 121
Stocks, 26, 27, 28, 29, 31, 32, 46, 49, 70, 74, 75, 102
  in Ford Motor Company, 120
  shareholders, 50, 82, 98, 102, 103, 104, 105–106
  stock market crash, 121
Stock tickers, 29–30, 84(box)
Stoppage, 44
Strikes, 98, 115, 117
Supply and demand, 55. *See also* Demand
Supreme Court, 119
Sweat equity principle, 98
Swift, Gustavus, 35, 39(box), 48–49, 59–60, 116
Swift, Louis, 48, 60
Swift and Company, 60

Takeovers, 75
Talent, hiring/retaining, 70–71, 72(box), 93–96
Tarbell, Ida, 42
Technology, ix, xi, 1, 6, 7, 22, 35, 68
Telecommunications, 74
Telegraphy, 1, 6, 11
Telephones, 6, 11–13, 115–116, 119–120
Television, 121
Theories, 10
Thinking, 76–77, 79
Tires, 15, 28, 38, 60

Trademarks, 63
Transportation, 35, 48. *See also* Railroads
Trust funds, 110
Twain, Mark, 10(box), 13

Urban areas, 2, 19
U.S. Steel, 92, 110, 117

Vail, Theodore, 12–13
Vanderbilt, William H., 69, 99
Vanderbilt, William K., 107(box)
Venture capital, 22, 29
Vertical integration, 44, 50
Vested interests, 6
Violence, 97, 117
Vision, 8–13, 33, 90, 92

Wages, 104(box). *See also* Incomes
Wal-Mart, 53, 55
Walton, Sam, 53
Wanamaker, John, 57(box)
Ward, A. Montgomery, 18–19, 67, 91, 115
Waste products, 38–40
Watson, Thomas A., 119
Watson, Tom, Sr., 91
Wealth, 106–110, 118
Wells, H. G., 43(box)
Western Union Telegraph, 12
Westinghouse, 16, 120
Wholesalers, 54
Winton, Alexander, 15
Wireless transmissions, 118, 121
Workforce, ix, 98, 99. *See also* Employment
Work, Wealth, and Happiness of Mankind, The (Wells), 43(box)
World War I, 16, 119, 120
Wozniak, Stephen, 23(box)
Wright brothers, 117–118
Wrigley, William, Jr., 56–57, 78–79

Xerox PARC, 13, 23(box)

Yankee of the Yards (L. Swift), 48, 60
Yes-men, 93